BEWARE THE PRETENDERS

JOHN MACARTHUR, JR.

This book is designed for your personal
reading pleasure and profit. It is also intended for group study. A leader's guide
with helps for teachers is available from
your local Christian bookstore or from the
publisher at 95¢.

VICTOR BOOKS

a division of SP Publications, Inc.

WHEATON, ILLINOIS 60187

Offices also in Fullerton, California • Whitby, Ontario, Canada • Amersham-on-the-Hill, Bucks, England

Scripture versions used in this book are the *New American Standard Bible* (NASB), © 1960, 1962, 1968, 1972, 1973 by The Lockman Foundation, La Habra, California; the King James Version (KJV); the *New International Version* (NIV), © 1978 by The New York International Bible Society. All quotations used by permission.

Recommended Dewey Decimal Classification: 227.9
   Suggested Subject Headings: JUDE; APOSTASY

Library of Congress Catalog Card Number: 79-93013
ISBN: 0-88207-798-8

VICTOR BOOKS
A division of SP Publications, Inc.
P.O. Box 1825 • Wheaton, Illinois 60187

CONTENTS

INTRODUCTION

The world is in a mess—and it doesn't seem to be getting any better. This should not surprise us though, for the Apostle Paul warned Christians over 1,900 years ago: "But realize this, that in the last days difficult times will come. For men will be lovers of self, lovers of money, boastful, arrogant, revilers, disobedient to parents, ungrateful, unholy, unloving, irreconcilable, malicious gossips, without self-control, brutal, haters of good, treacherous, reckless, conceited, lovers of pleasure rather than lovers of God; holding to a form of godliness, although they have denied its power!" (2 Tim. 3:1-5)

What an incredible and timely description of our day—it reads like the morning headlines or the evening news summary!

Paul also warned of another development that would occur in the last days: "But the Spirit explicitly says that in later times some will fall away from the faith, paying attention to deceitful spirits and doctrines of demons" (1 Tim. 4:1).

This "falling away" or "departure from the truth" is called *apostasy*—and it too is widespread in our day. Many people who were once attracted to Christianity are drifting away without ever making a genuine commitment to Christ Himself. Sometimes they actually leave the church, but in other instances they seek to remain in the mainstream of church life though they no longer be-

5

lieve in the basic truths of Christianity. These are the apostates about whom Jude warns us; they are the *pretenders*.

- They *pretend* to speak for Christ, but deny His deity and reject His lordship.
- They *pretend* to believe the Bible, but deny its inspiration, reject its authority, and pervert its teachings to suit their own preconceived ideas.
- They *pretend* to serve God, but in reality are serving their own selfish interests and desires.

What distinguishes apostates from other false teachers is that apostates *claim* to be Christian. *Apostasy is an inside job*—that's why it is so dangerous. Spiritual warfare would be so much simpler if all the enemies of the church were outside the church, but our ranks have been infiltrated by traitors (Jude 4) who are working for our defeat and destruction.

Jude writes to warn us about these apostates and to describe their characteristics in detail so that we will be able to recognize them.

The Book of Jude is a survival manual for Christians living in times of apostasy. This often-neglected book clearly sets forth the character of apostasy and apostate people. No other book gives Christians such a clear picture of how God wants them to live when they find themselves in the midst of widespread apostasy.

1. SECURITY OF CHRISTIANS

Jude, a bond-servant of Jesus Christ, and brother of James, to those who are the called, beloved in God the Father, and kept for Jesus Christ: May mercy and peace and love be multiplied to you.
Jude 1-2

In a parody of Rudyard Kipling's poem "If," someone has written: "If you can keep your head when all about you are losing theirs, you probably don't understand the situation." But Jude shows us how to fully understand the difficult times in which we are living, without being shaken by them.

In these opening verses, Jude greets the Christians to whom he is writing. Though this epistle is quite short, every word is filled with significant meaning. Even his greeting packs a powerful message to Christians living in the midst of apostasy and is worth examining word by word.

The name *Jude* is actually, in the Greek, "Judas." But because that name is associated with the betrayer of Christ, Bible translators have consistently used "Jude" instead. As Maxwell Coder notes, "Men call their sons Paul or Peter, they call their dogs Nero or Caesar, but the name *Judas* has been blotted out of our language except as a synonym of apostasy and treachery."

Jude calls himself "the servant of Jesus Christ, and brother of James." There are at least five men in the New Testament named Judas or Jude. To determine who *this* Jude is, let's go through a process of elimination.

Judas Iscariot, the betrayer of Christ, can be eliminated. So can Judas of Damascus (Acts 9:11) and Judas Barsabbas (Acts 15:22), for there is no indication that either of these men was the "brother of James."

Fourth is the other apostle named Judas, who is sometimes referred to as "Judas (not Iscariot)" (John 14:22) and also called Lebbaeus and Thaddaeus. In the King James Version of Luke 6:16 and Acts 1:13, he is said to be "the brother of James." However, the Greek construction in these verses is better translated "son," and the new Bible translations so translate it. This Judas, then, was the *son* of a man named James, not his brother.

The fifth Judas named in the New Testament was the half brother of the Lord Jesus. Matthew 13:55-56 says: "Is not this the carpenter's son? Is not His mother called Mary, and His brothers, James and Joseph and Simon and Judas? And His sisters, are they not all with us?"

The Roman Catholic Church, seeking to preserve its doctrine of Mary's perpetual virginity, identifies these family members as "cousins."

However, the Greek word used for these half brothers and sisters of Jesus is *adelphos*, which means "coming from the same womb." These were children born to Mary and Joseph *after* Jesus' birth. They were His half brothers and sisters because Jesus was virgin born. They had the same mother but not the same father.

We know very little about Joseph and Simon, but we know a great deal about James. He became the leader of the Jerusalem Church (Acts 15:13-21; 21:15-18; Gal. 2:9) and he wrote the New Testament Epistle of James. All that we know of Judas is that he was the brother of James and the half brother of Jesus. And because he is the only Judas in the New Testament who is identified as the "brother of James," we conclude that he is the writer of this epistle.

Many have wondered why he did not simply identify himself as "Judas, the brother of Jesus and James," but the answer to that question sheds light on Jude's character. Had he referred to himself as "the brother of Jesus," Jude could have been accused of boasting. Also, Jude may have been ashamed of the kind of brother he was to Jesus during His earthly life. Remember that the death and resurrection of Christ had the effect of changing, in a radical way, all the people who were physically related to Jesus. While growing up with Jesus, His brothers apparently developed some feelings of resentment toward Him, and during His ministry even ridiculed Him. John describes their mocking of Him on one occasion and ends by saying, "For not even His brothers were believing in Him" (John 7:5).

On another occasion, while Jesus was surrounded by a crowd to whom He was speaking, He received a message that His mother and brothers were waiting for Him outside. They had come "to take custody of Him, for they were saying, 'He has lost His senses'" (Mark 3:21). Jesus responded: "Who are My mother and My brothers? . . . For whoever does the will of God, he is My brother and sister and mother" (vv. 31-35). Jesus was saying to them that they could continue to think of Him as a family member for a time, but all of that would soon have to change.

We do not know exactly when Jesus' brothers and sisters were converted, but it may have been soon after His resurrection. Paul tells us that after Jesus was raised from the dead, He appeared to James (1 Cor. 15:7). And we know Jesus' brothers and sisters were with the apostles in the Upper Room following Jesus' ascension (Acts 1:14). But whenever the transformation took place, it produced dramatic changes. Jesus was no longer the resented half brother; He became to them Saviour, Redeemer, and Holy God.

Rather than using his unique relationship with Jesus in a way that would gain prestige for himself, Jude humbly describes his relationship to Christ in the same way as any other Christian might: "a servant of Jesus Christ." Then Jude also mentions his relationship to James, thereby identifying himself to his readers; for any Christian reading his epistle would recognize James as the well-known leader of the Jerusalem church.

After Jude properly introduces himself, he then characterizes the Christians to whom he is writing. He uses four terse phrases, each of which carries great theological and doctrinal meaning.

Christians are "the called ones," "the beloved ones," "the kept ones," and also "the blessed ones."

Brief as it is, this Epistle of Jude contains a heavy and sobering message which, if misunderstood, could have produced great fear among Christians. So Jude begins and ends his letter with strong statements on the security of true believers. In his opening sentence, Jude says they are "the called, beloved in God the Father, kept for Jesus Christ," and blessed with "mercy and peace and love." How much more secure could believers be! And if that is not enough, he concludes with a reminder—God is able to "keep you from stumbling and to make you stand in the presence of His glory blameless with great joy" (Jude 24).

In 2 Peter 2, which parallels the message of Jude in many respects, we see two striking examples of how God protects and delivers the godly who find themselves living in an ungodly culture doomed to destruction. Peter tells us that God "did not spare the ancient world, but preserved Noah, a preacher of righteousness, with seven others, when He brought a flood upon the world of the ungodly, and ... He condemned the cities of Sodom and Gomorrah to destruction by reducing them to ashes ... [but] rescued righteous Lot" (vv. 5-7). Peter's conclusion from this is that "the Lord knows how to rescue the godly from temptation, and to keep the unrighteous under punishment for the day of judgment" (v. 9). God is able to punish the guilty while at the same time preserving the innocent.

The Called Ones
The Christian has a divine call from God. His salvation is not something he dreamed up on his

own; it is an act of God.

The importance of this fact is demonstrated in that the word translated "called" is placed at the very end of the sentence, separated from its article which is near the beginning. According to the rules of Greek grammar, this places great emphasis on the idea of "calling."

Jesus issued a call when He said, "Come to Me, all who are weary and heavy-laden, and I will give you rest" (Matt. 11:28). On another occasion He stood up at the Feast of Tabernacles in Jerusalem and cried out: "If any man is thirsty, let him come to Me and drink" (John 7:37). A similar call is found in the last chapter of the Bible: "And the Spirit and the bride say, 'Come.' And let the one who hears say, 'Come.' And let the one who is thirsty come; let the one who wishes take the Water of Life without cost" (Rev. 22:17).

This general call can be resisted, however. When a person hears it with his physical ears, he can refuse to respond to it. When people hear the Gospel preached, they ought to receive it; they ought to obey it. But each person has a choice—he can receive Christ or reject Him.

Jesus told a parable about a man who prepared a big feast and then sent his servant to announce to those who had been invited, "Come, for everything is ready now." The invited guests represented the nation of Israel, and the man who invited them to his feast represented God. But the invited guests began to make excuses; one man had bought a piece of land, another had bought some oxen, and yet another had been recently married. All were too busy with other things to come to the feast. So the servant returned to his master, reporting that none of the invited guests were coming. The parable is a picture of Israel rejecting the call of God (cf. Luke 14:16-24).

We see this general call being resisted in other places in Scripture. Jesus said: "O Jerusalem, Jerusalem, who kills the prophets and stones those who are sent to her! How often I wanted to gather your children together, the way a hen gathers her chicks under her wings, and you were unwilling" (Matt. 23:37). Jesus told the Jewish leaders, "You are unwilling to come to Me, that you may have life" (John 5:40).

Stephen said to the leaders of Israel, "You men who are stiff-necked and uncircumcised in heart and ears are always resisting the Holy Spirit" (Acts 7:51). And his audience, as if to confirm the truth of Stephen's words, stoned him to death (vv. 58-60).

The author of Hebrews issues a stern warning against those who reject God's call: "See to it that you do not refuse Him who is speaking. For if those did not escape when they refused him who warned them on earth [that is, Moses], much less shall we escape who turn away from Him who warns from heaven" (Heb. 12:25).

There are two responses to this general call. Though from the divine side, this call is a sovereign act of God, from the human side, each individual has a choice of accepting or rejecting the truth of the Gospel when he hears it.

Those who respond to this call by trusting Jesus Christ as their Saviour are the ones whom Scripture designates as "the called." Paul addresses the Christians at Rome as those "who are beloved of God in Rome, called as saints" (Rom. 1:7). To the

Corinthians Paul writes: "But we preach Christ crucified, to Jews a stumbling block, and to Gentiles foolishness, but to those who are the called, both Jews and Greeks, Christ the power of God and the wisdom of God" (1 Cor. 1:23-24).

The Bible identifies people who are chosen by God, who hear the call of the Gospel and respond to it, as "the elect." This efficacious call which results in salvation is further described in 2 Thessalonians 2:13-14: "But we should always give thanks to God for you, brethren beloved by the Lord, because God has chosen you from the beginning for salvation through sanctification by the Spirit and faith in the truth. And it was for this He called you through our Gospel, that you may gain the glory of our Lord Jesus Christ."

In Revelation 17:14 we read, "Those who are with Him [Christ] are the called and chosen and faithful."

If you are a Christian, it is because you heard the truth of the Gospel and responded to the call of God. This concept of God's calling is truly beautiful. The Bible teaches us that we have been:

- called to fellowship with the Son (1 Cor. 1:9),
- called to inherit a blessing (1 Peter 3:9),
- called to freedom (Gal. 5:13),
- called to peace (1 Cor. 7:15),
- called to holiness (1 Peter 1:15),
- called to a worthy walk (Eph. 4:1),
- called to one hope (Eph. 4:4),
- called to eternal glory (1 Peter 5:10).

All of these—and more—are involved in the call of God that brings about salvation. If God has called us to eternal glory, we can be sure He will bring us there. "Faithful is He who calls you, and He also will bring it to pass" (1 Thes. 5:24).

The Beloved Ones

Another securing factor for believers, and one of the most fantastic things to realize, is that we are loved by God. This verb "beloved" (in Jude 1) is a perfect participle in the Greek, and means that God loved us at a point of time in the past *with continuing results*. It is in the strongest Greek verb tense, and indicates something which cannot be changed.

In the timeless past, before we were even born, God loved us. He set His affections on us and then demonstrated that love at Calvary when He sent the Lord Jesus Christ to die as our Substitute (Rom. 5:8). He fully manifested that love to us the day we came to Him, and He forgave our sins. It is an exciting thing to realize that God truly loves us!

Jesus said, "If anyone loves Me, he will keep My word; and My Father will love him, and We will come to him, and make Our abode with him" (John 14:23). "For the Father Himself loves you, because you have loved Me, and have believed that I came forth from the Father" (John 16:27).

God the Father loves Christians just as much as He loves Christ. Jesus prayed, "I in them, and Thou in Me, that they may be perfected in unity, that the world may know that Thou didst send Me, and didst love them, even as Thou didst love Me" (John 17:22-23).

John exclaims, "See how great a love the Father has bestowed upon us, that we should be called children of God" (1 John 3:1). God's love for

Christians is so incredible that John cannot find words to adequately describe it. God loves rebellious sinners enough to make them His children.

One of the biggest problems with adoption in our society is that there are so many "unadoptable" children that the agencies do not know what to do with them. When God adopted His children, He took plenty of "unadoptables" into His family. Not one of us was at all worthy to be in His presence, but He loved us so much that He took us in *forever*.

God's love is permanent. "For I am convinced that neither death, nor life, nor angels, nor principalities, nor things present, nor things to come, nor powers, nor height, nor depth, nor any other created thing, shall be able to separate us from the love of God, which is in Christ Jesus our Lord" (Rom. 8:38-39). The Father will always love us the same because He always loves Christ—and He sees us in Christ.

God has said: "I have loved you with an everlasting love; therefore I have drawn you with lovingkindness" (Jer. 31:3).

Nothing can separate us from the love of God! We are secure in the midst of apostasy. Heresy may flood the world, but Christians need not be shaken by it. The church may become a confusing mixture of true and false, but God knows His own (2 Tim. 2:19).

At a time in Israel's history when King Ahab and his pagan wife Jezebel had led most of the nation into Baal worship, the Prophet Elijah bemoaned the apostate condition of the nation. Filled with self-pity and discouragement, Elijah announced to God: "I have been very zealous for the Lord, the God of hosts; for the sons of Israel have forsaken Thy covenant, torn down Thine altars and killed Thy prophets with the sword. And I alone am left; and they seek my life, to take it away" (1 Kings 19:10, 14).

Elijah felt certain he was the only faithful one left in the entire nation. But God, in predicting the judgment He would bring on the nation for its rejection of Him, pointed out to Elijah: "Yet I will leave 7,000 in Israel, all the knees that have not bowed to Baal and every mouth that has not kissed him" (v. 18).

The Lord knew exactly how many were faithful to His love. And they would be protected and preserved in the midst of His judgment on the apostate nation.

This thought leads directly to Jude's next description of Christians.

The Kept Ones

In addition to being "called" and "loved," Christians are also "kept." The Greek word *tereo* means to "watch" or to "stand guard over." It stresses vigil and care, a real commitment to guard and keep something, to cherish it as one would a priceless treasure.

In Jude 1, the words "Jesus Christ" are in the Greek dative case which can be translated in several different ways. I believe the best translation in this verse is "*by* Jesus Christ." He is the One who keeps us, and we are as secure as His strength and power can make us.

Jesus Himself said: "I give eternal life to them; and they shall never perish, and no one shall snatch them out of My hand. My Father, who has given

them to Me, is greater than all; and no one is able
to snatch them out of the Father's hand. I and the
Father are One" (John 10:28-30). If we have doubts
about being able to keep our salvation, then we
are actually doubting the power of God.

Many passages in the New Testament speak of
God's keeping power. Near the end of his life Paul
wrote, "The Lord will deliver me from every evil
deed, and will bring me safely to His heavenly
kingdom" (2 Tim. 4:18).

Paul could be confident of this because Jesus
had prayed: "Holy Father, keep them [believers]
in Thy name. . . . I do not ask Thee to take them
out of the world, but to keep them from the evil
one" (John 17:11, 15). One of the significant truths
here is that since Jesus never prayed outside the
will of the Father, and since God's will must be
accomplished, Christians will be "kept" by the
power of God.

The author of Hebrews tells us *how* Jesus keeps
us: "He is able to save forever those who draw
near to God through Him, since He always lives
to make intercession for them" (Heb. 7:25). Jesus
is right now continually before the Father to plead
our case and to intercede for us. When Satan comes
before God the Father to accuse Christians, Jesus
is there to defend us and to declare that His death
on the cross paid the penalty for *all* our sins (cf.
1 John 2:1-2).

"For Christ did not enter a holy place made
with hands, a mere copy of the true one, but into
heaven itself, now to appear in the presence of
God for us" (Heb. 9:24). What an incredible picture: Jesus Christ appearing in the presence of
God *for us*!

Not a single one of Satan's charges can hold up in the heavenly court when Jesus stands before the Father and represents our case. The forgiveness of our sins has already been accomplished through the death of Christ, and now He lives in heaven as our divine Representative. We are forever "kept" through His interceding work on our behalf. We are truly secure in Him.

The Blessed Ones

Christians are also made secure through the blessings which God constantly showers on them. Jude mentions three of these blessings: mercy, peace, and love (v. 2).

1. God's mercy. If anything could cause us to lose our salvation, it would be sin; but whenever we sin, God *multiplies* His mercy to us (cf. Rom. 5:20). God is "rich in mercy" (Eph. 2:4). He created believers to be recipients of His mercy: "that He might make known the riches of His glory upon vessels of mercy, which He prepared beforehand for glory" (Rom. 9:23).

Some vessels are created to hold plants and others to hold water, but God especially designs Christians as vessels into which He can pour His mercy. We are, in turn, to display and dispense the mercy of God (Jude 22-23).

The Lord urges us to receive this mercy, which is always freely available to us. "Let us therefore draw near with confidence to the throne of grace, that we may *receive mercy* and find grace to help in time of need" (Heb. 4:16).

God makes His mercy and grace *abundantly* available to us through Christ (note the word "multiplied" in Jude 2), and He is eager for us to draw near to Him and receive them whenever we need them.

2. *God's peace.* Peace is another blessing God gives us. If we are misled by false teaching and begin to doubt our salvation, God multiplies for us His peace. Jesus said, "Peace I leave with you; My peace I give to you" (John 14:27). Not only does He *give* us peace, but "He *Himself* is our peace" (Eph. 2:14). Christ lives within us, and when we acknowledge His presence in our lives, we are filled with His peace. Paul writes, "Now may the God of hope *fill* you with all joy and peace in believing" (Rom. 15:13).

When we are troubled or anxious about something, we should admit it to God in prayer. When we do this, "the peace of God, which surpasses all comprehension, shall guard your hearts and minds in Christ Jesus" (Phil. 4:7).

God's desire is that we might be filled with His peace in all that we do. "Now may the Lord of peace Himself continually grant you peace in every circumstance" (2 Thes. 3:16).

3. *God's love.* The third blessing God multiplies to us is love. John reminds us, "In this is love, not that we loved God, but that He loved us and sent His Son to be the propitiation for our sins" (1 John 4:10). And again, "We love, because He first loved us" (v. 19).

We are able to truly love God—and others— only because God gives us His love. Paul tells us, "The love of God has been poured out within our hearts through the Holy Spirit who was given to us" (Rom. 5:5). "Poured out" is another perfect tense verb in the Greek, indicating permanence and lasting results.

Whether we lack mercy, peace, or love, God is continually multiplying these blessings to us. We are secure in Him because He takes up the slack whenever we are lacking. So in this outpouring of God's blessings, there is additional evidence of the believer's security.

No Need to Fear

Apostasy is present in the world and in the church—and it will get worse. These are not easy times in which to live. Christians are surrounded by everything which opposes the lifestyle God desires us to follow. Pressures and temptations to apostatize are on every hand, but Christians have no need to fear. We are secure in Jesus Christ, and He will not lose any of us.

But Satan is clever and may even tempt us to feel that our security in Christ allows us to sin without fear of serious consequences. This is false thinking. In the same passage in which Paul speaks of our security, "The Lord knows those who are His" (2 Tim. 2:19), he adds, "Let everyone who names the name of the Lord abstain from wickedness."

We are called, beloved, kept, and blessed by God—and our response should be to live in holiness and gratitude, for the One who has done so much for us deserves nothing less!

2. DESCRIPTION OF APOSTATES

Beloved, while I was making every effort to write you about our common salvation, I felt the necessity to write to you appealing that you contend earnestly for the faith which was once for all delivered to the saints. For certain persons have crept in unnoticed, those who were long beforehand marked out for this condemnation, ungodly persons who turn the grace of our God into licentiousness and deny our only Master and Lord, Jesus Christ.

Jude 3-4

In these verses Jude describes how he began writing an epistle on the important topic of salvation, only to be strongly impressed to change the thrust of his message and to urge his readers to contend for the faith in the midst of growing apostasy. The change was not motivated by Jude's lack of interest in his original subject. In fact, in attempting to write to them about salvation, he was "making every effort." The Greek word used here is a strong one, indicating powerful desire or purpose. The present tense of the verb also points to his concern—he had a continual, constant desire to write to them about the salvation which all Christians share in common.

While he was pursuing that goal, something happened which suddenly made it even more urgent for Jude to instruct believers to stand firm against apostasy. The Holy Spirit intervened in Jude's plans and put "pressure" on him so that he "felt the necessity" to exhort believers to contend for the faith.

Jude was so sensitive to the guidance of the Spirit that he quickly forsook his own project in order to follow the Spirit's direction. Jude does not tell us specifically *how* the Holy Spirit led him to change his writing plans, but it is possible that he received word of the growing influence of false teachers in the Christian community, perhaps in a specific local church, or in a group of churches.

As a shepherd who loved his people (he refers to them three times in this epistle as "beloved"), Jude would have been roused to action by such a message. All of his pastoral instincts would have sensed the urgency to protect the Christian flock from imminent danger. So he set about to prepare them for spiritual battle—to equip them to be able to discern the true from the false and to stand firmly against those who had departed from the truth.

Jude urged his readers to "contend earnestly," meaning they were to "fight with great strength, to defend strenuously." All Christians, throughout their lives, are in a war for the purity of the Christian faith—the "once-for-all-delivered-to-the-saints faith."

While there are many different Christian denominations, there is only one faith. "*The* faith" refers to the content of Christianity, the revelation of God, the whole body of teaching that makes up God's Word. And this revelation was delivered "once for all" in the past and is complete in the Bible. No new revelation is being added; the content of "the faith" was finalized at a point of time in history and is unchangeable. One of the clearest marks of a false cult is that it adds to or distorts the plain teaching of the Bible.

The Greek word for "contend" is the root of the English word "agony," and originally related to a stadium or place of athletic competition. Every day of our Christian lives is like the final competition for the gold medal at the Olympic Games. "Fight the good fight of faith," Paul urged young Timothy (1 Tim. 6:12). "I have fought the good fight, I have finished the course, I have kept the faith," Paul wrote in his last letter to his son in the faith. (2 Tim. 4:7).

The Nature of Apostasy

As Christians commit themselves to contend for the faith against the foe of apostasy, it is crucial for them to know the nature of the enemy. Since apostates who infiltrate the church do not announce themselves as apostates, it is important to know how to recognize them. Knowledge and discernment are needed to detect these wolves disguised in sheep's clothing.

A good place to begin is with Jesus' Parable of the Sower in Luke 8. The seed, representing the Word of God, fell on different kinds of soil, with differing results. Explaining the parable to His disciples, Jesus said: "And those on the rocky soil are those who, when they hear, receive the Word with joy; and these have no firm root; they believe for a while, and in time of temptation fall away" (Luke 8:13).

An apostate is someone who receives the Word of the Gospel, who superficially believes it for a time, and then falls away. His is a head knowledge, accepting the facts intellectually without ever making them personal. He *knows* the truth without *applying* it. He "accepts" God's revelation as true, but never makes a genuine commitment to it.

Something else in Jesus' parable helps us understand the nature of apostasy. Those represented by the rocky soil receive the Word with joy, and the Greek word for "receive" is *dechomai*. When Mark speaks of the good ground which brought forth fruit (Mark 4:20), the word for "receive" is *paradechomai*—a more intensive form of the same word. The good soil received the seed, or the Word, not superficially but deeply. Those people who are represented by the good soil take the Word deep down into their hearts where it becomes firmly rooted.

The distinction between these two verbs indicates a difference in how these two groups of people "receive" the Word—one superficially and intellectually, the other deeply and personally. Those who apostatize never bring forth the genuine fruit which is the evidence of true salvation.

Jude says apostates are "without fruit, doubly dead, uprooted" (v. 12).

Apostasy should not be confused with mere indifference to God's Word. This is an important distinction. Apostasy is not indifference or outright unbelief, though it may end up that way. Apostasy is involvement with the Word or intellectual acceptance of it that is only a pretense.

Remember, apostates in this context are *pretenders*. They claim to love Christ, but do not obey Him. They pretend to serve God, but really serve their own selfish desires. Most churches have at least a few people like this, who know God's revelation but refuse to make it their own.

If such people become teachers or preachers, they distort the teachings of Scripture (either knowingly or unknowingly) and lead astray those who ignorantly follow them. Jude is chiefly concerned with apostates who are in positions of influence in the church.

The writer of Hebrews says of these apostates: "How much severer punishment do you think he will deserve who has trampled under foot the Son of God, and has regarded as unclean the blood of the covenant by which he was sanctified, and has insulted the Spirit of grace?" (Heb. 10:29)

Paul speaks of those who "did not receive the love of the truth so as to be saved" (2 Thes. 2:10). They received the truth, but they never loved it sufficiently to commit their lives to it.

Simon the sorcerer, in Acts 8, is a dramatic example of an apostate. He "believed" and was baptized (v. 13); and, as he followed Philip around, was thoroughly amazed at the miracles the apostles were performing. Simon was present when

Peter and John laid hands on the people who had received the Word but had not yet received the Holy Spirit. When he observed that the power of the Holy Spirit was bestowed through this laying on of hands, he tried to buy the power with money. Simon's mercenary offer showed him for what he really was, a superficial follower who had failed to make a true commitment to Christ. Peter replied:

> May your silver perish with you, because you thought you could obtain the gift of God with money! You have no part or portion in this matter, for your heart is not right before God. Therefore, repent of this wickedness of yours, and pray the Lord that if possible, the intention of your heart may be forgiven you. For I see that you are in the gall of bitterness and in the bondage of iniquity (Acts 8:20-23).

Simon was an apostate—a pretender! He had never really put his faith in Christ even though he had been baptized. Because he had believed on an intellectual level only, he needed to repent and allow God to change his heart.

Apostasy Throughout the Bible

Apostasy surfaces in many places throughout the Bible, and the Greek noun and verb forms for "apostasy" are often used in the Greek Old Testament (called the Septuagint). The Israelites were warned, "Do not rebel against the Lord" (Num. 14:9). This word for "rebel" is the verb form of "apostatize." The people were urged not to abandon what they knew to be true.

In Joshua 22:16 we read: "Thus says the whole congregation of the Lord, 'What is this unfaithful act which you have committed against the God of

Israel, turning away from following the Lord this day, by building yourselves an altar, to rebel against the Lord this day?' " Apostasy is rebellion against the Lord whom a person *claims* to know and love. Apostates are the "pretend" people of God, who turn their backs on God. The Israelites did it again and again in the Old Testament.

In the New Testament, the word "apostasy" is used only twice. James confronted Paul in Jerusalem with these words: "They [the Jews in Jerusalem] have been told about you, that you are teaching all the Jews who are among the Gentiles to forsake [apostatize from] Moses, telling them not to circumcise their children nor to walk according to the customs" (Acts 21:21).

The only other time the word "apostasy" is found in the New Testament is in 2 Thessalonians 2:3: "Let no one in any way deceive you, for it [the end time] will not come unless the apostasy comes first, and the man of lawlessness is revealed, the son of destruction."

The *idea* of apostasy is seen many times in the New Testament, even when the word itself is not used. Some of Jesus' disciples "withdrew, and were not walking with Him anymore" (John 6:66). They turned their backs and walked away from Jesus, after believing in Him for a time.

Apostasy is also discussed in 1 John 2:18-23. A group of apostates had been in the church, but had now broken away from it. These people had in some fashion denied the Lord Jesus Christ (v. 22), and John says that their departure from the church shows that they never really belonged to it in the first place (v. 19). They never really knew Christ. They were *pretenders*!

Peter speaks of people who profess a knowledge of Christ and whose lives appear to be changed, but who then reject Christ and return to their old ways. He says: "If after they have escaped the defilements of the world by the knowledge of the Lord and Saviour Jesus Christ, they are again entangled in them and are overcome, the last state has become worse for them than the first" (2 Peter 2:20).

Paul warns Timothy about apostates in the pulpit and apostasy in the pew. Pastors and teachers in the church can show themselves to be false teachers.

The Spirit explicitly says that in late-times some will fall away from the faith, paying attention to deceitful spirits and doctrines of demons, by means of the hypocrisy of liars seared in their own conscience as with a branding iron, men who forbid marriage and advocated abstaining from foods, which God has created to be gratefully shared in by those who believe and know the truth (1 Tim. 4:1-3).

These false preachers, who fill many pulpits around the world today, use God-language and talk about Christ and promote "love," and yet God says they are "hypocritical liars." They are *pretenders*!

In addition to "pretenders" in the pulpit, we also have the problem of *phonies* in the congregation. These false church members are described in 2 Timothy 4:3-4:

For the time will come when they will not endure sound doctrine; but wanting to have their ears tickled, they will accumulate for themselves teachers in accordance to their own desires; and will turn away their ears from the truth, and will turn aside to myths.

A similar situation existed in Jeremiah's time. "The prophets prophesy falsely, and the priests rule on their own authority; and My people love it so!" (Jer. 5:31) The people actually *preferred* falsehood to truth and apostasy to faithfulness.

The reason many pastors and their people deny the inspiration of Scripture, the deity of Christ, His virgin birth, His literal resurrection, and His return is that they are apostate. They have the Bible in their hands and have read it, but they have turned their backs on the truths God has revealed. They are controlled by Satan.

Apostasy, or falling away from the truth, began in the Garden of Eden when Satan questioned the Word of God which Eve knew to be true: "Has God said?" and "You shall surely not die!" (See Genesis 3.) So Eve moved away from the truth of God by rejecting what she knew God had said. Unbelief was thus introduced, and apostasy in a primitive form had its beginning.

Cain rebelled against God's revelation concerning sacrifices. The people of Noah's day who heard his preaching for 120 years rejected the truth. Israel failed to enter the Promised Land under Moses and failed to conquer it completely under Joshua because they disbelieved the Word of God. Apostasy led to immorality in the time of the Judges and eventually to captivity in Assyria and Babylon. Also, apostasy blinded Israel to the credentials of her Messiah.

In certain periods of the church's history, apostasy has threatened the very life of the church. That threat has never been greater than it is today.

How Apostates Operate

Jude presents three significant aspects of apostates that give us insight into how they operate. Careful attention to what Jude says will not only help us recognize apostates, but will also enable us to more effectively fight against them.

1. Penetrating. Jude says certain men "crept in unnoticed" (v. 4). Apostates worm their way into churches, into seminaries and Christian schools, and into denominations—and eventually they weaken Christ's church through the false teachings they promulgate.

They are sneaky people who "clip in by the side door." In extrabiblical literature the word "apostate" was used to refer to a criminal who had been exiled from a country and was secretly slipping back into that country. The word was also used in a legal sense to describe someone who pleaded a case very cleverly and with guile.

These apostates are Satan's counterfeits who "go down into and alongside" real Christians in order to infiltrate and weaken the life and leadership of the church. Whereas the church is purified and strengthened under persecution, it suffers great damage from apostasy.

Jesus warned about apostates and false teachers: "Beware of the false prophets, who come to you in sheep's clothing, but inwardly are ravenous wolves" (Matt. 7:15). And Paul warned the Ephesians: "I know that after my departure savage wolves will come in among you, not sparing the flock" (Acts 20:29).

Peter describes apostates as "false teachers among you, who will secretly introduce destructive heresies, even denying the Master who bought them. . . . And many will follow their sensuality, and because of them the way of the truth will be maligned; and in their greed they will exploit you with false words" (2 Peter 2:1-3).

Peter predicted apostasy on a massive scale; and by Jude's time, only a few years later, this falling away from the truth had already begun. Men had already crept in secretly and had begun to corrupt the doctrine of the church and to unsettle the souls of believers.

2. *Predicted.* As we have just seen, the Bible predicts the nature of apostates and the manner of their operation. Jude says apostates "were long beforehand marked out [or written about] for this condemnation." The key word here is *progegrammenoi,* which means "prewritten." Jude says apostasy was written about—and condemned—long ago.

Apostasy should not take us by surprise, for God predicted, from the very beginning, that apostates would appear on the scene to work their destruction, and He also predicted their condemnation and punishment. Jude cites a prophecy by Enoch, in the seventh generation from Adam, that tells of God's judgment on apostates (Jude 14-15). We will examine that prophecy in some detail in chapter 5.

The point was that both long ago (in Enoch's time) and more recently (at the time of Peter's writing), as well as throughout the centuries in between, God had "prewritten" the condemnation of apostasy. No apostate could ever plead ignorance; God's verdict on apostasy was in long ago.

Isaiah 8:19-21 contains another powerful example of God's predictions concerning apostates:

And when they say to you, "Consult the mediums and the spiritists who whisper and mutter," should not a people consult their God? Should they consult the dead on behalf of the living? To the law and to the testimony! If they do not speak according to this Word, it is because they have no dawn. And they will pass through the land hard-pressed and famished, and it will turn out when they are hungry, they will be enraged and curse their king and their God as they face upward. Then they will look to the earth, and behold, distress and darkness, the gloom of anguish; and they will be driven away—into darkness.

Every time someone speaks in the name of God, we must evaluate his or her message by comparing it with God's Word. If a person's teaching willfully contradicts Scripture, we know that person's message is not from God and the person is giving false teaching. God does not deal lightly with those who distort His truth or teach contrary to His Word.

In Isaiah 47:9-15 the false teachers are astrologers who lead the people to worship the luminaries in the heavens. Today most astrologers could not technically be classified as apostates since they have not first come to a knowledge of the Christian faith. But the punishment of these astrologers, in the Book of Isaiah, is devastating—there will not be so much as ashes remaining.

Hosea describes the depravity of the false prophets and says that God "will remember their iniquity, He will punish their sins" (Hosea 9:9). And finally, in Zephaniah 3:1-8, God has strong language for apostate Jerusalem, ending with this powerful warning: "My decision is to . . . pour out on them My indignation, all My burning anger for all the earth will be devoured by the fire of My zeal" (v. 8).

So we see that apostasy has been written about in God's Word from the very beginning—and every time it is written about, it is condemned!

3. *Portrayed*. In portraying the truth about apostates and how they operate, Jude mentions their character, their conduct, and their creed.

Of their *character,* Jude says these apostates are "ungodly men" (v. 4, KJV), showing a total lack of reverence for God. The word translated "ungodly" actually means "impious" or "without worship."

These people talk about God, and may use pious words, but their hearts are far from Him. They may be in the church and claim to minister in the name of Jesus Christ, but they do not truly know Him. Like Simon Magus (Acts 8), they are in the church for what they can get out of it.

Concerning their *conduct,* Jude says they "turn the grace of our God into licentiousness." "Licentiousness," *aselgeia,* refers to "unrestrained vice" or "gross immorality." It describes a person so lost to honor, decency, and shame that he does not care who sees his sin and immorality. Not that he necessarily flaunts his sin, but that he simply does the most shameful acts, because he has ceased to care about shame or decency at all. He may even believe that since the grace of God is wide enough to cover any sin, then a person may sin as much as he likes and be forgiven for everything.

This is a perversion of God's grace, but it should not surprise us that some apostates think that way. As they fall away from the knowledge of the truth,

Satan easily blinds their minds to the moral and spiritual consequences of sin. They feel they can behave any way they like and still be covered by the forgiveness of God. Grace is twisted into a justification for sinning.

Paul's answer to the question "Shall we sin because we are not under law but under grace?" was an emphatic "God forbid!" (Rom. 6:15, KJV)

The *creed* of apostates, Jude says, denies "our only *Master* and *Lord, Jesus Christ.*" Apostates always deny the deity of Christ; they make Him merely a creature. This despicable false teaching, espoused by the cults and the liberals, strikes right at the heart of Christianity.

The word for "Master," is *despotēs*, from which we get the word "despot." It speaks of Jesus' complete and absolute sovereignty as Ruler of the universe. Apostates refuse to recognize Jesus as the God of the universe.

The word for "Lord," is *kurios*, which means a title of honor or distinction. Apostates refuse to honor Jesus as Lord and seek to bring Him down to human level.

The name "Jesus" identifies Him as Saviour, and "Christ" is the Greek equivalent of Messiah, the Anointed, the King of kings. Apostates deny it all—His sovereign rule as God, His lordship over believers as the One to be honored and obeyed, His saviourhood, and His messiahship.

Apostates will not escape judgment and condemnation for their denials. Jesus warned: "Whoever shall deny Me before men, I will also deny him before My Father who is in heaven" (Matt. 10:33). Paul repeated this warning: "If we deny Him, He also will deny us" (2 Tim. 2:12).

The character, conduct, and creed of apostates are summed up in Titus 1:16: "They profess to know God, but by their deeds they deny Him, being detestable and disobedient, and worthless for any good deed." Ungodly and irreverent in character, they disparage God's grace and deny the lordship of Christ.

How to Contend for the Faith

Living as we do in the midst of an age of apostasy which promises to become even worse, we must know *how* to contend for the faith and stand against the rising tide of false teaching. Here are some suggestions.

1. We must study and obey the Word of God ourselves. This is basic. Unless we know the truth, we will not be able to detect error; unless we obey the truth, we will not have the moral courage to stand against false teaching and apostasy.

2. We must give unflinching and unhesitating witness to the truth of God's Word. The Bible is under attack from many sides, and we must not only speak up in its defense but also proclaim its message of salvation through faith in Jesus Christ.

3. We can fight the battle against apostasy by supporting and encouraging faithful pastors and teachers who honor the Word of God and the Christian faith without compromise.

4. We can also fight for the faith by training more people for leadership in the church, so that they can defend the faith and teach others to do the same. We need to support churches, institutes, seminaries, and schools that teach people the Word of God and how to defend the faith.

Christians must not be afraid to enter the battle

against apostasy. We must contend for the truth of the Christian faith against the apostates and clever false teachers. And with God's help we will be victorious!

3. DESTRUCTION OF APOSTATES

Now I desire to remind you, though you know all things once for all, that the Lord, after saving a people out of the land of Egypt, subsequently destroyed those who did not believe. And angels who did not keep their own domain, but abandoned their proper abode, He has kept in eternal bonds under darkness for the judgment of the great day. Just as Sodom and Gomorrah and the cities around them, since they in the same way as these indulged in gross immorality and went after strange flesh, are exhibited as an example, in undergoing the punishment of eternal fire.

Jude 5-7

In American history the catchphrases "Remember the Alamo" and "Remember Pearl Harbor" were all it took to dredge up a flood of memories left over from highly charged military battles. More recently one simply warns, "Remember Vietnam," or "Remember Watergate," and people are suddenly reminded of events which held their attention for months and even years.

The purpose of such reminders is to warn us to stay on guard so we do not allow certain kinds of incidents to occur again. Part of the human decaying and dying process is that our memories, which once were sharp and clear, fade with time. We lose track of facts and emotions that we once thought we would never be able to forget.

Jude gives his readers a series of vivid reminders in these three verses. He jogs their memories with three quick warnings which immediately flood their minds with powerful pictures of God's judgment on man's sin:

- "Remember the Israelites in the wilderness!"
- "Remember the angels that sinned!"
- "Remember Sodom and Gomorrah!"

Each catchphrase represented its own detailed narrative of rebellion and unbelief. Jude's readers already knew the full story of these three situations, for they were described in their Scriptures. So they did not need a detailed account but simply a brief reminder of God's attitude toward apostasy. In case some of Jude's readers were being swayed by false teachers, they would be solemnly warned of their imminent danger.

Israel in the Wilderness
Jude first reminds them of the final end of the unbelieving Israelites who wandered 40 years in the wilderness. All Jews knew well the beautiful story of God's redemptive love demonstrated in the Exodus. Whenever anyone spoke of Jewish history, the Exodus was one of the things he talked

about. So Jude has no need to recount the whole story; he simply wants his readers to take note of two points: (1) God miraculously delivered *all* the Israelites out of Egypt, and (2) He destroyed those who apostatized. This is what Jude wants them to remember.

God had delivered His people "by a mighty hand and by an outstretched arm" (Deut. 4:34). In return, He wanted only their gratitude, affection, and trust. But within a few days, they began to grumble and complain—first about food, then about water, and later about the leadership of Moses and Aaron. And at the first opportunity, while Moses was away on Mt. Sinai receiving the Law from the very finger of God, the Israelites turned to idolatry (Ex. 32).

Finally, they arrived at the Promised Land of Canaan and actually rejected it because they feared its inhabitants and didn't trust in the God who had already brought them so far. They did not believe that the God—who had taken them out of Egypt, parted the Red Sea for them, drowned Pharaoh's army for them, and fed them with manna from heaven and water from the rock—could also win battles for them against the giants and fortified cities of Canaan.

The irony was that the Canaanites were quick to believe that the God of Israel could defeat them. Even 40 years later when Joshua's spies encountered Rahab in Jericho, Israel's enemies were still living in dread of the Israelites because of what the Canaanites had heard about Israel's God. So while Israel's enemies trembled with fear, the Israelites backed away and refused to fight—and complained that God had betrayed His people by even delivering them out of bondage (Num. 14).

That was it! God had finally had enough. He condemned them to wander in the wilderness for 40 years until all the members of the adult generation had died. Only Caleb and Joshua, the two spies who believed God would give them the victory, survived to enter Canaan. All the others were never allowed to enter the glorious land which they had rejected.

Jude is reminding his readers that God deals sternly with those who turn their backs on Him. The Israelites had every reason to believe God; He had proven Himself again and again in one incredible miracle after another. Yet they refused to believe Him.

The writer of Hebrews also points to these Israelites as an example of God's judgment on those who reject what they know to be true. In the audience to whom he wrote were the Jews who were wavering; they knew the truth of the Gospel but were threatened with persecution and were fearful of making a full commitment to Christ. To such people the writer of Hebrews addresses a stern warning. His point is: Do not do what the Children of Israel did! Freed from bondage in a foreign land and ready to enter the Land of Promise God had specially prepared for them, they died instead in the wilderness *because they did not believe God*. (See Hebrews 3:7-19.)

God swore in His wrath that they would not enter His rest (Heb. 3:11). God said:

Surely all the men who have seen My glory and My signs, which I performed in Egypt and in the wilderness, and yet have put Me to the test these 10 times and have not listened to My voice, shall by no means see the land which I swore to their fathers, nor shall any of those who spurned Me see it (Num. 14:22-23).

The final exhortation in Hebrews 4:1-2 is to believe in God. They had heard the truth, but they needed to join themselves to it by faith.

In one brief phrase Jude, in effect, says to his readers, "Remember the Israelites who died in the wilderness because of unbelief!" His readers were reminded of God's judgment poured out on a rebellious people. They were reminded that they too would experience God's wrath and judgment, if they turned away from Him.

Angels Who Sinned

Jude's second reminder concerns certain angels "who did not keep their own domain, but abandoned their proper abode." Attempts to understand the meaning of this verse have produced three views of just who these angels were. The first view is that this verse refers to some falling away of angels about which we have no information. The basic problem with this view is that Jude indicates he is simply *reminding* his readers about something of which they already have full knowledge. Also, the incidents in verses 5 and 7 are both from Scripture, so it is likely that this incident is also taken from Scripture.

The second view considers this event to be the original fall of Satan and his demons. The problem with this view is that the angels referred to in Jude are presently "kept in eternal bonds under darkness for the judgment of the great day" (v. 6). However, Satan and his demons are obviously loose today and actually are ruling over their dominion on the earth during this present age.

The third view recognizes these angels as those beings mentioned in Genesis 6 who cohabited with human women and brought forth a strange new race of half-angel and half-human beings.

The angels to whom Jude refers "did not keep their own domain." The word "domain" *archēn* may mean rule, principality, dignity, or domain, but probably "rule" is the best definition perhaps indicating the angels divinely appointed function. These creatures did not keep to the high position or domain given them by God. Instead they "abandoned" their habitation; the verb tense *(aorist)* refers to a point in time, indicating a specific act. At some specific point, they deliberately rebelled and left their dwelling place and what was consistent with their character and nature. They turned their back on the place and function God had assigned to them, thus becoming apostates.

The transition into the next verse provides a clue as to what it was these angels did. Verse 7 begins with "just as," pointing to a certain similarity between the sin of these angels and the sin of Sodom and Gomorrah. Those cities, according to verse 7, "indulged in gross immorality and went after strange flesh." Sodom and Gomorrah participated in gross immorality "in the same way as these," and in the Greek grammatical construction, "these" can refer only to the angels in the previous verse.

So the angels also gave themselves to gross immorality. The usual Greek word for immorality or fornication is *porneuō,* from which we get the word *pornography;* but the word used here in Jude is *ekporneuō,* an intensified form of the word. So the immorality with which we are dealing here is of an unusual or intensified nature.

Those angels did not keep to their own domain, but abandoned the proper abode God had designed for them and gave themselves over to a gross kind of sexual evil, just as Sodom and Gomorrah did. The men of those two cities lusted after the angelic beings who had come to visit Lot. And if the angels in verse 6 had the same kind of perverted lust for strange flesh, then they must have lusted after humans. The word for "strange" in verse 7 is *heteros,* meaning different in nature or kind.

Since Jude is reminding his readers of a situation with which they are already familiar, we need to look for such an incident described in Scripture, and we find it in Genesis 6:1-4:

> Now it came about, when men began to multiply on the face of the land, and daughters were born to them, that the sons of God saw that the daughters of men were beautiful; and they took wives for themselves, whomever they chose. Then the Lord said, "My Spirit shall not strive with man forever, because he also is flesh; nevertheless his days shall be 120 years." The Nephilim were on the earth in those days, and also afterward, when the sons of God came in to the daughters of men, and they bore children to them. Those were the mighty men who were of old, men of renown.

In support of this view, it should be noted that in the Old Testament angels are several times referred to as "sons of God" (Job 1:6; 2:1; 38:7). The Greek translation of the Old Testament, the Septuagint, translates this phrase in Genesis 6 as "angels." Nowhere in the Old Testament, with the single exception of Hosea 1:10, is the term "sons of God" used for God's people. The phrase is most often used to refer to something brought into existence by the direct creative act of God. Men are thus not called "sons of God" until they have been *recreated* in Jesus Christ.

Historically, Genesis 6 was interpreted as a reference to angels, as Josephus makes clear in his history of the Jewish people. The early church also held that view until the fourth century when some people began to interpret Genesis 6 as referring to children of Seth.

These fallen angels had sexual relations with women and produced a race of mighty creatures who were some mixture of demon and man. And one reason God brought the Flood was to destroy this half-breed race.

The main objection some people have to this interpretation of Genesis 6 is that Jesus taught that in the resurrection, people neither marry nor are given in marriage "but are like angels in heaven" (Matt. 22:30), who do not marry or have sexual relationships.

But Jesus was speaking of the holy angels who remained "in heaven" under God's dominion. He was not talking about fallen angels who had been cast out of heaven to roam about the earth as wicked spirits.

Jesus was also referring to the fact that in and of themselves, angels cannot procreate. But angels are able to take the form of a human body, as evidenced by the angelic men who visited Abraham and Sarah, and later Lot (Gen. 18—19). In fact, in the Old Testament whenever angels took on human form, they appeared as males. The Bible never says that angels are sexless. Jesus was talking about holy angels in heaven and their inability to procreate. He was not referring to the possibility that fallen angels could take on human bodies and unite with humans.

God brought terrible judgment on these evil creatures who left the angelic realm and took on male human bodies to procreate with human women. He "has kept" *tēreō* them in eternal bonds since that time. The verb is a Greek perfect tense, indicating these fallen angels were put away at a time in the past and are continually "kept," or guarded. They were confined by God in the past and they are still confined today in chains.

They are also kept "under darkness." This word for "darkness" *zophos* is used only here and in Hebrews 12:18 and 2 Peter 2:4, 17, and indicates terrible, deep, dense black.

Peter also speaks of the same incident involving these angelic beings and links it to the time of Noah: "God did not spare angels when they sinned, but cast them into hell and committed them to pits of darkness, reserved for judgment; and did not spare the ancient world, but preserved Noah, a preacher of righteousness, with seven others, when He brought a flood upon the world of the ungodly" (2 Peter 2:4-5).

"Spirits in prison" are also linked with the time of Noah in 1 Peter 3:18-20:

> For Christ also died for sins once for all, the just for the unjust, in order that He might bring us to God, having been put to death in the flesh, but made alive in the spirit; in which also He went and made proclamation to the spirits now

in prison, who once were disobedient, when the patience of God kept waiting in the days of Noah, during the construction of the ark, in which a few, that is, eight persons, were brought safely through the water.

This passage also provides a clue as to what Jesus did between the time He died on the cross and the time He was raised from the dead. While His body was in the tomb, His spirit went to preach to the spirits in prison. But He did not preach the Gospel *euaggelizō*; He made a proclamation *kē-russō*, announcing His triumph over sin, over death, and over Satan himself.

Peter describes these imprisoned ones as spirits who were disobedient during the days of Noah. So these evil angels, the same ones mentioned in Jude 6, have been confined to some unknown place of terrible blackness awaiting the great Judgment Day when God will pass final judgment on them.

Jude warns his readers to remember these angels who were created with a dignity worthy of their high position, but who turned from their Creator and went their own way into gross immorality. They knew God and had experienced heaven, yet they turned away. And God did not take lightly their sin and wickedness, but brought on them a terrible judgment of blackness and bondage proclaimed by Christ who descended to their prison at His death—a judgment which is only a prelude to an even greater judgment.

Sodom and Gomorrah
Though the people of Sodom and Gomorrah seem in some respects to be unlikely prospects for *apos-*

tasy, there is reason to believe that these people did *know* the truth of God. The destruction of these cities probably occurred about 450 years after the Flood, when at least one of Noah's sons, Shem, (Gen. 11:10-11) would have been still living. Since this was about 100 years after Noah's death (Gen. 9:28), people would have known about his years of preaching God's truth. They would likely have even known of the sin of the evil angels and the resulting race of half-breeds which God had destroyed.

The story of Sodom and Gomorrah's sexual perverseness is recorded in Genesis 19. Two angels who had taken the form of men came to visit Lot in Sodom, where he lived with his family. When Lot saw the angels, he bowed to the ground and offered them the hospitality of his home. They reluctantly accepted his invitation to dine with him and to spend the night in his home.

But before they retired for the evening, Lot's house was suddenly surrounded by all the men of the town, both young and old, who demanded that Lot send his guests outside. The men of Sodom wanted to have sexual relations with them. Frightened at the prospect of having his divine guests attacked in his home, Lot did a strange thing—he offered his virgin daughters to the men in place of the angels.

When the men of the city threatened Lot and pushed forward to break down the door of his house, the angels pulled Lot inside and struck the wicked attackers with blindness. Then the angels announced to Lot that they had come at God's command to destroy the city because He would tolerate its evil no longer.

Even after being struck blind, the men of Sodom continued to attack Lot's house in an effort to have homosexual relations with his two visitors. God, in His righteous anger, wiped Sodom and Gomorrah and their sister cities off the face of the earth.

There are at least 23 different passages in the Bible which allude to the destruction of Sodom and Gomorrah. The destruction was a strong reminder of God's judgment on sin, and a graphic example for Jude to use.

Why Do People Apostatize?

In reviewing three such powerful examples of God's judgment on apostasy, we might wonder how those who have the truth of God so clearly laid out for them can turn away from it. The Bible suggests reasons why people apostatize:

1. *Persecution.* Some people are not willing to pay the price. They know the definition of a Christian, but they are not willing to step over the line and be counted for Christ. Jesus clearly warned His followers that they would suffer persecution (Matt. 24:9).

2. *False teachers.* When someone understands the Gospel and is on the verge of making a commitment to Christ, Satan often confuses him with appealing but false doctrine (Matt. 24:11-12).

3. *Temptation.* Some people receive the Gospel intellectually and then Satan showers them with temptations until they are drawn away by their lusts (Luke 8:13).

4. *Worldliness.* People can be drawn away by the attraction of the world and by an acceptance of the world's values (2 Tim. 4:10).

5. *Neglect.* Some people reject God's love and grace simply by ignoring what they know to be true (Heb. 2:3).

6. *Hardened hearts.* Some people turn away from God's truth by hardening their hearts against it, again and again, until it is too late (Heb. 3).

7. *Religion.* Some people get just enough religion to become immune to the real thing. They taste the heavenly gift and get some idea of the powers of the age to come. They become involved on the fringes of Christianity, and this limited involvement is just enough to pacify them (Heb. 6:1-6).

8. *Forsaking assembling with Christians.* This refusal to come together can be detrimental to the true believer as well as to someone close to believing, and can lead to apostasy. (See Hebrews 10:25.)

These reasons help us understand why some people apostatize, but there is never a legitimate excuse for apostasy. And God is never tolerant of it!

Apostasy Today

God has not changed since the days of the Old Testament apostasies cited by Jude. He is no more tolerant of apostasy now than He was then. In fact, the writer of Hebrews teaches that God's judgment on apostasy since the death of Christ is even more severe than it was before:

> For if we go on sinning willfully after receiving the knowledge of the truth, there no longer remains a sacrifice for sins, but a certain terrifying expectation of judgment, and the fury of a fire which will consume the adversaries. Anyone

who has set aside the Law of Moses dies without mercy on the testimony of two or three witnesses. How much severer punishment do you think he will deserve who has trampled under foot the Son of God, and has regarded as unclean the blood of the covenant by which he was sanctified, and has insulted the Spirit of grace? For we know Him who said, "Vengeance is Mine, I will repay." And again, "The Lord will judge His people." It is a terrifying thing to fall into the hands of the living God (Heb. 10:26-31).

If God's punishment was severe to Israel in the wilderness, to the angels who sinned, and to Sodom and Gomorrah, how much worse punishment will there be for the person who knows the truth of Jesus Christ and tramples underfoot His precious blood of the New Covenant!

God is dealing with apostasy now more severely than He did because now apostasy involves a rejection of His Son, Jesus Christ. Nothing that happened in the Old Testament could even begin to compare with the seriousness of rejecting God's Son, Jesus Christ. "If any man does not love the Lord," declared the Apostle Paul, "let him be accursed" (1 Cor. 16:22).

And God will judge such sin without showing any favoritism. If He showed no special favor to any of the apostates in the three illustrations cited by Jude, He will certainly show no special favor to those who reject His own Son.

If you know the truth but have not yet made a commitment to it, be warned. Today is the day of salvation—do not delay any longer; do not neglect such a great salvation.

4. CONDUCT OF APOSTATES

Yet in the same manner these men, also by dreaming, defile the flesh, and reject authority, and revile angelic majesties. But Michael the archangel, when he disputed with the devil and argued about the body of Moses, did not dare pronounce against him a railing judgment, but said, "The Lord rebuke you." But these men revile the things which they do not understand; and the things which they know by instinct, like unreasoning animals, by these things they are destroyed. Woe to them! For they have gone the way of Cain, and for pay they have rushed headlong into the error of Balaam, and perished in the rebellion of Korah.

Jude 8-11

In a century when people have become numb to the bizarre and the cruel and are almost unshockable, people sat stunned as they watched news broadcasts from Guyana where hundreds of bodies of Jim Jones' cult members lay dead and bloated. One of the largest mass suicides in history left more than 900 dead, including the cult leader himself.

Jim Jones had put up a great front for years. Blacks and whites alike rushed to join his movement and became fiercely loyal to him. Jones professed to be a Christian and preached from the Bible regularly. Local authorities believed in his work so thoroughly that they even committed youths who were wards of the court into Jones' care.

But facts that had not seeped out before his death began to pour out after the mass suicide scene. Jones was a sexually depraved man who demonstrated heinous cruelty to those around him, showing no respect for the commands and authority of God. He was motivated by greed and self-glorification.

Jones' character and conduct are a living example of an apostate who becomes a false teacher. Jude, in verses 8-11, describes these evil men who lead others astray. He portrays the conduct of these apostates and also the kind of company they keep.

Conduct of Apostates

We have noted the conduct of apostates of the past about whom Jude reminded his readers: the Israelites in the wilderness, the angels who sinned, and the sexually immoral Sodom and Gomorrah. Now Jude describes some of the characteristics of present-day apostates so that his readers might recognize these false teachers for what they really are.

Jude says these apostates are dreamers who defile the flesh, reject authority, and speak evil of glories. Physically, they are immoral. Intellectually, they are arrogant. And spiritually, they are blasphemers. These same three characteristics were evident in Jude's three Old Testament case studies. Sodom and Gomorrah defiled the flesh; the sinning angels rejected God's authority; and the Israelites in the wilderness spoke evil of God and complained against Him.

The nature of apostasy has not changed. Apostates of Jude's day behaved much as they had in Old Testament times, and they pursue the same evil course today. The amazing thing is that they continue their evil ways, even though they know what the Bible teaches about apostasy and how God has powerfully condemned it in the past. God declared to Israel, "I overthrew you as God overthrew Sodom and Gomorrah, and you were like a firebrand snatched from a blaze; yet you have not returned to Me" (Amos 4:11). Apostates never learn!

When Jude calls the apostates "dreamers" (v. 8, KJV), he does not use the word for dream *onar* which refers to purposeful or significant dreaming, as when God spoke to the Old Testament prophets through dreams. The word Jude uses, *enupniazomai,* means a confused state of the soul or an abnormal imagination, producing dreams in which the ego is controlled and held captive by ungodly, sensual confusion. The word carries the idea of arbitrary fancies from a perverted mind which is deaf to reality and truth. These false teachers are deluded and beguiled, and the "truth" they see in their dreams is, in reality, false.

All of us have had dreams that were so vivid

that they seemed real, and we were glad when we woke up. But these false teachers conjure up their own evil dreams and wish them to be real.

Jude characterizes the conduct of these dreamers in three ways:

1. They defile the flesh. Sooner or later most false teachers are exposed on a moral level. But even if they are not *publicly* exposed, Jude's characterization of them still stands. Interestingly, modern false teachers seem to gravitate to radio and television; perhaps it seems an easy way to raise funds without much personal scrutiny of your methods.

During the years when my dad was preaching on TV, we used to come into contact with some really seedy characters who had religious programs on the air. One man had several homosexual bodyguards, and he was as immoral as a man can be. His life would make a black mark on a piece of coal, and yet he still has his own television show today.

Another preacher often came to the TV studio too drunk to speak, and the announcer would have to read his sermon for him on the air. But whenever the preacher came in sober enough to give his message, he would make a big plea for money, and checks to keep him on the air would pour in. Finally, he was found murdered in a hotel, and the whole sordid story of his vice and immorality became public knowledge.

Only the Holy Spirit can control fleshly desires, and false teachers do not have God's Holy Spirit abiding in them (Jude 19). No matter how carefully the apostate false teacher tries to maintain a moral front, the moral consequences of his actions will usually become visible—at least to those who know him well. Occasionally, an exception comes along. Satan keeps his man morally clean in order to put up a good front and deceive even more people.

The word for "flesh" in Jude 8 is *sarx*; and the word for defile, *miainō*, means to spot or stain. At first it meant to stain by bloodguiltiness, but it later came to mean any kind of stain. When connected with *sarx, miaino* usually means sexual immorality.

The whole second chapter of 2 Peter is given over to a description of false teachers, and one thing that stands out is the immoral quality of their lives. "And many will follow their *sensuality*" (v. 2); "those who *indulge the flesh* in its corrupt desires" (v. 10); and "speaking out arrogant words of vanity, they entice *by fleshly desires, by sensuality*" (v. 18). Peter mentions these apostates again later (3:3) and says, "Know this first of all, that in the last days mockers will come with their mocking, *following after their own lusts.*"

We need to be warned about these people because on the surface they often seem so nice. People caught up in the cults often are very friendly, but God does not want us to be deceived by appearances. Under their pretty surfaces often lurk filthy immoralities. Jim Jones is a graphic reminder of this.

2. They show contempt for authority. A second characteristic of these dreamers is their arrogance and their contempt for authority. The word "reject" *atheteō* means to reject or do away with something that has been established. The "authority" they are rejecting is *kuriotēs*, which is taken from the word for "lord." They reject lordship, including the lordship of Jesus Christ.

The word can refer to several kinds of authority, including civil government or national leaders. About this Maxwell Coder says:

> Jude 8 supplies a key to the otherwise inexplicable fact that apostate religious leaders are often found associated with subversive organizations which seek to overthrow the authority of the United States. Not until the tide of apostasy began to rise during the 20th century was there any serious effort to set aside the dominion of the government which our fathers established (*Jude: The Acts of the Apostates,* Moody, 1967, p. 54).

While apostates resist all kinds of authority, they mainly *rebel against Christ.* False teachers reject the lordship of Christ and pursue their own desires. This behavior should not surprise us, since apostates are agents of Satan, and Satan seeks to undermine every authority God has established— the home, the government, the church.

Jude has already mentioned that apostates "deny our only Master and Lord, Jesus Christ" (v. 4). While using it for their selfish ends, they also resist the authority of the Word of God and water down or twist its teachings to suit their own preconceived ideas. They disregard what the Bible teaches about coming judgment on those who do not obey the truth of God's Word.

3. They speak blasphemies. Apostates are also characterized by speaking evil of glories. "Revile" *blasphēmeo* is the Greek word from which we get "blasphemy." The verb is a continuous present, indicating apostates are *continually* blaspheming.

They are speaking evil about literal "glories" *doxa*. Though the word is sometimes translated "angels" or "angelic majesties" (as in the NASB of v. 8), *doxa* is never properly used to speak of angels. I believe "glories," as it is used here, refers to the glories of Christ and of God.

Apostates in word or in lifestyle really speak evil of Christ; they deny His deity, His virgin birth, His miracles, His atoning death, His resurrection, and His second coming.

Jude cites the example of Michael, the archangel, contending with Satan for the body of Moses. Rather than hurling a railing accusation against the devil, Michael simply said, "The Lord rebuke you." Michael never stepped out of bounds, and he was in the position of chief angel. Michael did not contend with Satan on the basis of his own position or power, but deferred to the Lord's power and judgment in the situation.

It is always wrong to pronounce a "railing judgment" (or a "slanderous accusation," NIV) against someone in authority. And if Michael would not speak evil of Satan, how much more should we not speak evil of governmental authorities, church leaders, and especially of God Himself! In fact, the Apostle Paul urges Christians to "speak evil of no man" (Titus 3:2, KJV).

This brief reference to a dispute over the body of Moses is the only place in Scripture where the incident is mentioned. There is no way to know the full significance of the dispute, since no further information is given, but I believe Satan was trying to prove he had a right to Moses' body because Moses had been a murderer (Ex. 2:12).

It is interesting to consider why Satan may have

wanted possession of Moses' body. Since Moses was venerated by the Jews, I believe Satan would have used Moses' body as an object of worship—in much the same way as people today worship "pieces of the cross" and other religious relics. Just think how Satan could have embalmed Moses' body and urged people to worship it. This is just one more of Satan's methods for getting people hooked on idolatry. But God was not about to allow such a gross thing to happen, so He sent Michael to bury Moses' body (cf. Deut. 34:5-6).

Jude goes on to point out (v. 10) that these false teachers also revile and speak evil against things which they do not understand. Talking to an apostate is like talking to a person who is having a dream. Have you ever tried to carry on a conversation with a person who is talking in his sleep? He makes no sense because he does not really understand; he has no idea what you are talking about. Just so, the "natural man does not accept the things of the Spirit of God; for they are foolishness to him, and he *cannot* understand them, because they are spiritually appraised" (1 Cor. 2:14).

Apostates are spiritually blind and deaf. Peter says of them: "But these, like unreasoning animals, born as creatures of instinct to be captured and killed, reviling where they have no knowledge, will in the destruction of those creatures also be destroyed" (2 Peter 2:12).

While I was a student in seminary, I had many opportunities to speak at youth camps. I will always remember one particular denominational summer camp. As I listened to their entertainment and preliminaries before I was to speak, I noticed that their material was really not in good taste. In fact, some of it bordered on being crude.

So I made a quick decision that my first message to them would be on the authority of the Word of God. I spoke as powerfully as I knew how on why the Bible is authoritative and how we know it is the revelation of God—not realizing that the leaders of those college students did not believe in the authority of Scripture.

Afterward, one of the leaders was furious. He yelled at me, "I can't believe that you are stupid enough to believe the Bible." (That's an exact quote.) I was shocked, but told him I certainly did believe it and that I would continue to teach that way if they wanted me to stay the rest of the week. If they wanted me to leave, I would do so.

The leaders met together and after much discussion decided I should stay because they might receive a bad reaction from some of the more conservative groups represented there. But they were determined to allow me to speak only in the evenings. So in the mornings a missionary who did not fully believe the Bible would speak, encouraging young people toward the mission field.

Finally, 30 of the young people signed a petition and gave it to the director of the conference, saying, "We would like to know what the message is we're supposed to give once we get to the mission field. Would you please have Mr. MacArthur speak in the mornings also?"

The leaders initially refused; but the movement grew until the students were boycotting the morning meeting, and the leaders finally asked me to speak in the mornings also.

It was an exciting time, and by the end of the

week, dozens of people had become believers. They shared their testimonies about how God had changed their lives once they recognized the authority of His Word.

Those leaders never invited me back to their camp. In fact, they never spoke to me again. But what that leader said to me about being stupid for believing the Bible has always stuck with me. He was reviling something about which he had absolutely no understanding. He was like a man mumbling in his sleep, who could not begin to comprehend the reality of the situation confronting him.

Although apostates criticize what they *do not* understand, Jude states that they are corrupted or destroyed by what they *do* understand. About this point Michael Green says:

> If a man is persistently blind to spiritual values, deaf to the call of God, and rates self-determination as the highest good, then a time will come when he cannot hear the call he has spurned, but is left to the mercy of the turbulent instincts to which he once turned in search of freedom. And those instincts, given free reign, are merciless. Lust, when indulged, becomes a killer (*Second Epistle General of Peter and the General Epistle of Jude,* Eerdmans, 1968).

The word for "unreasoning" (v. 10) is *alogos.* *Logos,* of course, means "word," and the alpha prefix on the word negates *logos* so that the meaning of *alogos* is "senseless" or "ignorant." These apostates, like senseless animals, are consumed and destroyed by the very lusts they seek to fulfill. The things that apostates *do* know about are the things that continue to damn them. Jude's summary comment on these false teachers is, "Woe to them!" (v. 11) They will perish eternally in their own corruption.

Company of Apostates

We all know that you can tell a lot about a person by the company he keeps. Jude mentions three apostates from the Old Testament and points out that they represent the kind of company which present-day apostates keep. These three are among the host of apostates who can be traced back to the early days of man's history.

The company of apostates includes Cain, who shows the error of false religion; Balaam, who demonstrates the greed and seductiveness of apostates; and Korah, who shows the apostates' rebellion and open blasphemy against God. There are also three progressive stages of action here: They *go* in the way of Cain; they *rush* headlong into the error of Balaam; and they *perish* in the rebellion of Korah.

To go in the *way* of Cain is to reject the right way. To rush after the *error* of Balaam is to reject the *truth*. And to *perish* in Korah's rebellion is to reject *life*. What we have here then is the antithesis of John 14:6, for Jesus said, "I am the Way, and the Truth, and the Life; no one comes to the Father, but through Me." Instead of committing themselves to Christ, who is the Way, the Truth, and the Life, these apostates have rejected God's way for the way of Cain, God's truth for the error of Balaam, and God's life for the death of Korah.

1. The way of Cain. Both Cain and Abel (Gen. 4) brought offerings to the Lord. I believe God had told them that He wanted an animal sacrifice. But

Cain chose to determine the kind of offering he would bring, and he brought the fruit of the ground. God required a blood sacrifice, but Cain rejected God's way, and acted in unbelief. (See Hebrews 11:4.) He rejected God's revelation and did what he wanted to do. Because of this, his offering was unacceptable to God.

Apostates today resemble Cain in his rejection of the required blood sacrifice. One of the main tenets of liberalism is rejection of the death of Christ as an atonement for sin. Liberals refuse to view His death as substitutionary. They say Christ's death is an example of a martyr dying for a cause.

Because God refused Cain's offering, "Cain became very angry and his countenance fell" (Gen. 4:5). Cain turned against God. He departed from the truth and became an apostate. And since behavioral evil usually accompanies false doctrine, the first thing Cain did when he turned away from God was to kill his brother Abel.

Modern apostates follow in the footsteps of Cain by rejecting God's way of salvation. They prefer to go their own way.

2. The error of Balaam. The story of Balaam, an interesting character who was an Old Testament prophet for hire, appears in Numbers 22—25. As the Israelites prepared to enter Canaan, their arrival was viewed unhappily by Balak, king of nearby Moab. So he offered Balaam a large sum of money to come and to curse Israel.

Balaam found himself in a real dilemma, because he wanted the money but he feared God enough to know that there could be real danger in cursing Israel when God had not told him to do that. Even Balaam's donkey knew his master was stepping out of line (Num. 22:21-35).

Nevertheless, Balaam tried several times to pronounce a curse on Israel. Each time, however, a blessing came from his lips. King Balak was most displeased (24:10).

So Balaam, realizing he would not be able to curse Israel, devised a plan to get God to curse Israel (cf. 31:16; Rev. 2:14). Balaam instructed the women of Moab to seduce the Israelite men and to get them to worship pagan gods. Then God wo ld punish the Israelites for their immorality and idolatry. And his plan worked exactly as he had plotted it (Num. 25:1-9).

Balaam got his way in bringing God's judgment on the Israelites, but he was also destroyed in the process. We read in Numbers 31 that the Israelites "killed the kings of Midian along with the rest of their slain. . . . They also killed Balaam the son of Beor with the sword" (31:8). These all were killed because they "caused the sons of Israel, through the counsel of Balaam, to trespass against the Lord in the matter of Peor" (31:16).

Balaam was available to the highest bidder, and apostates usually are motivated by money. Some of the men pastoring liberal churches, teaching false doctrine in apostate seminaries, "preaching" on TV and traveling the country asking people to send in money for their needy ministries, pay themselves handsome salaries and have become wealthy off other people. They are in the ministry for the money.

Peter warns pastors not to shepherd the flock of God "for sordid gain" (1 Peter 5:2). And he says of these false teachers, "In their greed they will exploit you with false words" (2 Peter 2:3).

3. *The rebellion of Korah*. Korah's rebellion, described in Numbers 16, was against the leadership of Moses and Aaron. Korah, a fellow Levite, felt that he and all the other Israelites were holy before the Lord, and thus they did not need Moses and Aaron to be mediators between them and God. So Korah, along with three other men, led 250 elders of Israel in rebellion against God's appointed leaders.

God brought a powerful and dramatic judgment against these men. The ground opened up and swallowed Korah and his cohorts and their households. Then fire from the Lord consumed the 250 men who had supported Korah's rebellion.

Korah is a classic example of the person who believes he does not need a Saviour. He believes he is good enough and does not think he needs a Mediator, but can go to God for himself. He rejects God's arrangements and tries to do things his own way.

But Jesus said, "No one comes to the Father, but through Me" (John 14:6). And Paul reminds us that "there is one God, and one Mediator also between God and men, the Man Christ Jesus (1 Tim. 2:5).

Korah's rebellion was blasphemy against the holy character of God, as if mortal man could conceivably enter the very presence of God without a Mediator. There must be Someone who has first taken care of the sin-barrier which separates man from God.

These men represent three classic illustrations of apostasy: Cain, rejecting a redemptive blood sacrifice; Balaam, choosing what would pay the most and bring the greatest material rewards; and Korah, rejecting his need for a Mediator. And once again we see that there are fearful judgments awaiting those who know the truth and reject it. All three of these men knew the truth and chose to move away from it—and their lives ended in fear, violent death, and divine judgment.

5. RECOGNIZING FALSE TEACHERS

These men are those who are hidden reefs in your love feasts when they feast with you without fear, caring for themselves; clouds without water, carried along by winds; autumn trees without fruit, doubly dead, uprooted; wild waves of the sea, casting up their own shame like foam; wandering stars, for whom the black darkness has been reserved forever. And about these also Enoch, in the seventh generation from Adam, prophesied, saying, "Behold, the Lord came with many thousands of His holy ones, to execute judgment upon all, and to convict all the ungodly of all their ungodly deeds which they have done in an ungodly way, and of all the harsh things which ungodly sinners have spoken against Him." These are grumblers, finding fault, following after their own lusts; they speak arrogantly, flattering people for the sake of gaining an advantage.

Jude 12-16

Apostate false teachers are often pretenders—that is what makes them so dangerous. They disguise themselves to look like one of us so they can infiltrate the church, create confusion and dissension, and lead the unwary astray.

In spite of their clever "disguises," these false teachers always bear certain marks or characteristics which give them away. Jude is warning Christians that they must be alert to *recognize* these characteristics and not be deceived by the disguises.

True Character of Apostates

To describe the character of these wicked false teachers, Jude draws analogies from the realm of nature—rocks, clouds, trees, the sea, and stars— to illustrate the spiritual truths he desires to communicate.

1. Hidden rocks. Jude describes these apostates as hidden "rocks" or "reefs" in the love feasts of Christians. The word *spilades* here means "sunken rocks" or "hidden reefs" which, while hidden from view can run a ship aground and destroy it.

In the early church, Christians met together regularly to share the Lord's Supper and have a meal together which was known as the "love feast." In that culture, as in many cultures today, there was no middle class, only the very rich and the very poor. Many of the Christians in the first century were slaves who did not have a great deal to eat, so the love feast was an occasion for the rich to share their abundance with the poor. For a slave, it might be the only really good meal he would have all week, and he would look forward to the meal as if it were truly a "feast."

In the beginning, the rich people brought, out of their abundance and the poor people brought, out of their scarcity, and they all came together to share their food and their love for the Lord and for each other. However, by the end of the first century, the love feast, which had begun so beautifully, deteriorated through dreadful abuses.

In the first-century church at Corinth, these feasts had become drunken orgies. The rich would bring their own food for the meal and eat it themselves without sharing with the poor. The wealthy formed cliques and associated only with certain people. During the feasts some ate and drank too much, while others had little or nothing. For the Christians in Corinth, the meaning of the love feast was being destroyed.

The apostates in the church were like feelingless rocks in these love feasts. They perverted the feasts for their own ends, and used them to promote immorality. It is important to remind ourselves that these apostates were not merely spectators watching the feast through the windows. They were in the church, and, as active participants in the feasts, exerted a strong influence on how the feasts were conducted.

What should have been a unique time of Christian fellowship, and a powerful witness to pagan neighbors, became instead an ugly sore in the church. Before long the church had to abandon the love feast altogether because it had become so badly abused.

Jude says of these apostates, "They feast with you without fear, caring for themselves" (v. 12). These selfish people came to the love feasts and gorged themselves with no concern for anyone else. Apostates "care for" themselves; the verb is *poimainō*, which is related to the word for "shepherd." These people "shepherd" *themselves* and take care of only their *own* needs. As false shepherds, who are really wolves in disguise, they participate in the life of the church to fulfill their own desires, and to gratify their own lusts.

2. *Clouds without water.* Jude also describes these apostates as "clouds without water." Clouds are generally viewed as a promise of rain, so these false teachers are seen as people who make promises they cannot fulfill. They claim to have answers, and often persuade others that they do. But they are really pretenders with no solutions to offer.

"Like clouds and wind without rain is a man who boasts of his gifts falsely" (Prov. 25:14). Apostates boast of great gifts to offer their followers, but they are false, empty people, driven with no direction or purpose.

The word translated "without water" *anudros* is used in Matthew 12:43 to refer to the waterless places where evil spirits abound. The waterless clouds in Jude are "carried along by winds." Perhaps there is a connection here between these apostates and unseen evil spirits who control them. False teachers are empty, useless, unstable, under the influence of demons—people who promise much but provide nothing of value.

3. *Trees without fruit.* Apostates are next characterized as "autumn trees without fruit." Just as trees lose their leaves and become dry and barren in autumn, apostates are devoid of spiritual life and fruit. They are "doubly dead, uprooted." Jesus said, "Every plant which My heavenly Father did

not plant shall be rooted up" (Matt. 15:13). These trees are uprooted because they bear no fruit and are therefore useless. Because apostates and false teachers have no spiritual life in them, what they teach can never bring spiritual life or growth to others.

These fruitless trees are reminiscent of Jesus' parable in Luke 13:6-9:

A certain man had a fig tree which had been planted in his vineyard; and he came looking for fruit on it, and did not find any. And he said to the vineyard-keeper, "Behold, for three years I have come looking for fruit on this fig tree without finding any. Cut it down! Why does it even use up the ground?" And he answered and said to him, "Let it alone, sir, for this year too, until I dig around it and put in fertilizer; and if it bears fruit next year, fine; but if not, cut it down."

Almost all trees appear to be dead in autumn, but the ones that still have life in them will later bloom again and produce fruit. They only *appear* to be dead. However, these "twice dead" trees mentioned by Jude appear to be dead because they are dead! They will never produce any fruit.

4. Waves of the sea. Jude next likens these false teachers to "wild waves of the sea, casting up their own shame like foam" (v. 13). In the Bible the sea is frequently used as a symbol of those who do not know God. "The wicked are like the troubled sea, when it cannot rest, whose waters cast up mire and dirt" (Isa. 57:20, KJV).

If you've ever taken a walk along the shore of a polluted river or lake, you can readily understand the picture Jude is painting here. The water, which should be for cleansing and purifying, becomes foul and continually deposits only foam and scum on its beaches. In the same way, false teachers serve only to stir up shameful deeds, religious harlotry, false doctrine, and lies against God's truth.

5. *Wandering stars.* Jude climaxes his description of these false teachers by comparing them to "wandering stars, for whom the black darkness has been reserved forever." Since most stars move in precise and fixed orbits, Jude is here speaking of shooting stars which make a sudden flash and then are gone. The word translated "wandering" *planētēs* is related to the word translated "error" in verse 11. Like these false, erratic stars which flash across the sky in brilliance for a moment and then disappear into an eternal night, false teachers also rise and fall. In a few brief moments of brightness, they attract many people to their false light, only to vanish suddenly into eternal darkness. What an awful, intense, indescribable hell—darkness forever!

Throughout the Bible, God is identified with light, and evil is associated with darkness. Jesus Christ is the Light of the world, and Christians are to walk in the light. But those who do deeds of darkness reject the Light.

God intended that there should always be a clear distinction between good and evil, light and darkness, and He judged those Old Testament priests and prophets who confused the two and called good evil and evil good (Isa. 5:20). He will also judge these apostates who are like shooting stars and thus counterfeits of the true Light of the world.

Each of Jude's word pictures from the natural realm points to a different aspect of these apostates or false teachers. Hidden rocks speak of the *danger* of apostasy. Waterless clouds refer to the *false promises* of false teachers. Autumn trees point to the apostates' *barrenness* and lack of anything fruitful to offer. Wild waves show their frenetic and *wasted effort*. And wandering stars picture their *brief and aimless course,* ending in blackness and darkness.

What apt descriptions! Maxwell Coder contrasts these word pictures of the apostates with a picture of Christ:

> One is reminded by way of contrast with the Lord whom these men deny. He is the Rock of our salvation; they are hidden rocks threatening shipwreck to the faith. He comes with clouds to refresh His people forever; these are clouds which do not even bring temporary blessing. He is a Tree of Life; these are trees of death. He leads beside still waters; these are like the restless troubled sea. He is the bright and morning Star, heralding the coming day; these are wandering stars presaging a night of eternal darkness (*Jude: The Acts of the Apostles,* p. 76).

If Christians are not continually on guard against the influence of apostates and false teachers within the church, these wicked people can gain a foothold before the church even knows what is happening. The Apostle Paul anticipated this evil influence within Christ's church when he warned the Ephesian elders:

> Be on guard for yourselves and for all the flock, among which the Holy Spirit has made you overseers, to shepherd the church of God which He purchased with His own blood. I know that after my departure savage wolves will come in

among you, not sparing the flock; and from
among your own selves men will arise, speaking
perverse things, to draw away the disciples after
them (Acts 20:28-30).

All churches must be continually on guard
against the evil subtlety of false teachers who infiltrate the church. They may appear suddenly,
without warning, and begin to stir up shame and
scum in the fellowship. Church leaders must
shepherd their flocks with much vigilance and with
love.

Final Condemnation of Apostates

Once again Jude emphasizes how long ago God
first condemned and judged apostasy. Jude quotes
from Enoch, who lived before the Flood. Enoch
had such deep communion with God while living
on earth that he never died, but simply walked on
into the presence of God (Gen. 5:24).

The words of Enoch's prophecy which Jude
quotes are nowhere else recorded in Scripture,
and some scholars believe the words are taken
from the apocryphal Book of Enoch. However, we
can be sure that the Holy Spirit guided Jude in
selecting accurate information, whatever its source.
If Jude says these words were spoken by Enoch
before the Flood, then we can rest assured that
they were.

(It should be noted that Jude's use of this quo-
tation from the Book of Enoch does not vouch for
the reliability of the entire Book of Enoch. The
same is true of the apocryphal book *The Assump-
tion of Moses* from which Jude may have taken
the information about Michael contending with
Satan. This specific information is accurate, but

Jude's use of it does not guarantee the reliability of the rest of the book.)

How incredible to think that the first prophecy given through a man concerned the second coming of Jesus Christ: "Behold, the Lord came with many thousands of His holy ones, to execute judgment upon all" (Jude 14-15). God Himself had prophesied (Gen. 3:15) that One would come who would bruise the serpent's head, but Enoch's prophecy is the first such given through a man.

It is interesting that the last prophecy in the Bible (Rev. 22:20) also concerns Jesus' second coming and His judgment. From beginning to end God has given prophecies about the return of Christ in judgment. This is a serious and important matter and God wants men to know about it.

Enoch's prophecy, recorded here by Jude, says that the Lord "came" with thousands of His holy ones. The verb is a Greek past tense which we call a prophetic past or a future past. The past tense can sometimes be used to refer to a future event because when the Greeks needed to state something that was *absolutely certain* to happen and could not be changed, they stated it as if it had already taken place.

Another example of this is found in Ephesians 2:6, where we are told that God has "seated us with Him [Christ] in the heavenly places." Our place with Christ in heaven is so certain that Paul states it in a past tense. Likewise, the second coming of Christ is so certain and unchangeable that God caused it to be stated in these verses in the past tense.

Enoch also prophesied that Christ would bring with Him "many thousands of His holy ones"

(v. 14). Who are these "holy ones"? Are they angels or redeemed people—or both?

Jesus said, "When the Son of man comes in His glory, and all the angels with Him, then He will sit on His glorious throne" (Matt. 25:31). But in Colossians 3:4 we read: "When Christ, who is our life, is revealed, then you also will be revealed with Him in glory." So it appears that holy angels and redeemed people will both be coming with Christ when He returns.

Enoch also tells us the purpose of Christ's return: "to execute judgment upon all" (Jude 15). The verb is a Greek infinitive of purpose *aorist*; Jesus is coming *for the purpose* of judgment. All rebels and unbelievers will be judged; no one will escape. The Lord Jesus came once in humility to bring salvation; He will come again in wrath to bring judgment.

The Apostle Paul describes Christ's return in judgment:

When the Lord Jesus shall be revealed from heaven with His mighty angels in flaming fire, dealing out retribution to those who do not know God and to those who do not obey the Gospel of our Lord Jesus Christ. And these will pay the penalty of eternal destruction, away from the presence of the Lord and from the glory of His power, when He comes to be glorified in His saints on that day, and to be marveled at among all who have believed—for our testimony to you was believed (2 Thes. 1:7-10).

When Christ returns, Christians will be glorified, but all others will be confronted with the flaming fires of judgment.

The result of Christ's judgment, according to

Enoch, will be "to convict all the ungodly." He will bring tremendous conviction in the lives of the ungodly for the deeds they have done and for the words they have spoken against Him.

These are *thoroughly* ungodly people, whose ungodliness is manifested in their attitude, in their speech, and in their actions. The verdict against them is found in Matthew 25:41: "Depart from Me, accursed ones, into the eternal fire which has been prepared for the devil and his angels."

Reaching an emotional climax in verse 16, Jude sums up his description of these vile false teachers: "These are grumblers, finding fault, following after their own lusts; they speak arrogantly, flattering people for the sake of gaining an advantage."

The word translated "grumblers" *goggustai* is used only here in the New Testament. In the Greek Old Testament (the Septuagint) the word is used to describe the murmurings of the Israelites in the wilderness. Just as the Israelites were continually grumbling and resisting, apostates are characterized by their complaining against the truth of God, discontent, sullen rebellion, and stubborn disobedience.

The word for "finding fault" *mempsimoiros* is a compound of two Greek words, one which means "to blame" and the other relating to one's allotted fate. So the word refers to complaining about one's lot in life.

The fallen angels were dissatisfied with their proper habitation. Israel was dissatisfied with God's care for them in the wilderness. Korah was dissatisfied with God-ordained mediatorship. Cain was dissatisfied with God's plan for sacrifice. Balaam was dissatisfied with God's will and wanted more money. In each case grumbling and complaining led to open rebellion and apostasy.

Morally, apostates "follow after" *poreuomai* their own lusts. This is a present tense verb, indicating that they *habitually* seek self-satisfaction guided by lust.

"They speak arrogantly." Anyone who has heard the verbosity of some modern apostate false teachers needs little comment on that phrase. They speak eloquently on social needs and on psychology—pompous palaver which, in the words of Shakespeare, is "full of sound and fury, signifying nothing." Empty words serve only to seduce the unwary.

These apostates also "flatter people for the sake of gaining an advantage." Speaking lies and half-truths, these false teachers eagerly flatter others in order to get something from them. Apostates always seek to gain favor with other people and seldom take a stand against popular opinion. These false teachers avoid God's truth in order to speak words that will be pleasing to their audiences.

Jesus' Judgment on Apostates

Jude, in quoting Enoch, points to Jesus as the One who is coming to execute fierce judgment on these apostates and false teachers. While modern man often denies the reality of hell and final judgment on the grounds that Jesus was so meek and mild and God the Father is all love and grace, the truth is that Jesus spoke more about hell than any other person in Scripture.

Several times in the Sermon on the Mount, Jesus spoke of the awful reality of hell, calling it "hell fire" (Matt. 5:22, KJV). He warned that a person's whole body could go into hell and that this hell was so awful that the loss of an eye or a hand was as nothing compared to it (5:30).

Later in the Sermon, Jesus warned that every tree not bearing good fruit would be cut down and thrown into the fire (7:19). He also said that those who do not believe in Him will be "cast out into the outer darkness; in that place there shall be weeping and gnashing of teeth" (8:12).

In urging His disciples to action and courage, Jesus said, "Do not fear those who kill the body, but are unable to kill the soul; but rather fear Him who is able to destroy both soul and body in hell" (Matt. 10:28). In Matthew 13:40-42 we have Jesus' prediction of the great final judgment:

Therefore just as the tares are gathered up and burned with fire, so shall it be at the end of the age. The Son of man will send forth His angels, and they will gather out of His kingdom all stumbling blocks, and those who commit lawlessness, and will cast them into the furnace of fire; in that place there shall be weeping and gnashing of teeth.

Jesus taught that hell is a place of torment and agony—"the unquenchable fire" (Mark 9:43). He also taught that hell will never end—"the eternal fire which has been prepared for the devil and his angels" (Matt. 25:41; cf. v. 46).

The word translated "hell" is *gehenna,* which was the name of the city dump outside Jerusalem where fires were kept continually burning to destroy the refuse from the city. Because the fires there were never allowed to go out, *gehenna* became the closest analogy available to teach that hell is both awful and eternal.

Jesus also taught that there will be degrees of torment in hell. He said to the cities of Galilee:

Woe to you. . . . For if the miracles had occurred in Tyre and Sidon which occurred in you, they would have repented long ago in sackcloth and ashes. Nevertheless I say to you, it shall be more tolerable for Tyre and Sidon in the day of judgment, than for you. . . . If the miracles had occurred in Sodom which occurred in you, it would have remained to this day. Nevertheless I say to you that it shall be more tolerable for the land of Sodom in the day of judgment, than for you (Matt. 11:21-24).

Thus the people who are in hell from Sodom will find it more tolerable there than the people in hell from the Galilean cities where Jesus performed most of His miracles.

The difference in the intensity of punishment is directly related to the amount of one's knowledge of the truth. Jesus points this out in a parable recorded in Luke 12:47-48:

And that slave who knew his master's will and did not get ready or act in accord with his will, shall receive many lashes, but the one who did not know it, and committed deeds worthy of a flogging, will receive but few. And from everyone who has been given much shall much be required; and to whom they entrusted much, of him they will ask all the more.

In summary, Jesus taught that there are two final destinies for people—heaven or hell. Hell is a dreadful place of separation, utter blackness, and eternal punishment which is compared to a raging fire that never goes out. Yet people will experience different degrees of intensity in hell, depending on how much knowledge of the truth they had in this life.

This is one reason Jude and other biblical writers speak so strongly against apostasy. Apostates will suffer more because they knew the truth and turned away from it. The hottest hell is reserved for those who knew the most and still rejected it.

The New Testament teaches the reality of hell, and the primary Teacher of that reality is none other than our Lord Jesus Christ.

Warnings to the Church

Hell will no doubt be far worse than anything the human mind can imagine. But just try to imagine what it would be like to be conscious in complete darkness forever. Even now in a momentary blackout of electrical power, people are struck with fear and panic.

Apostates, even when they sit in church week after week, are choosing darkness rather than light. In one sense, hell is simply an extension of the darkness which people have already chosen in this life by rejecting Jesus Christ, the Light of the world. At the final judgment they will be condemned to an eternity separated from that Light.

The Apostle Peter powerfully reiterates our Lord's teaching about the terror that hell will hold for apostates. After a lengthy and vivid description of those apostates who become false teachers, Peter warns that it will be worse for them because they once knew the way of truth and willfully turned away from it.

For if after they have escaped the defilements of the world by the knowledge of the Lord and Saviour Jesus Christ, they are again entangled in them and are overcome, the last state has become worse for them than the first. For it would be better for them not to have known the way of righteousness, than having known it, to turn away from the holy commandment delivered to them (2 Peter 2:20-21).

Jude's epistle is a stern warning to Christians and non-Christians alike. His desire for the person in the church who has never made a commitment to Christ is that he realize the dreadful judgment he will face because of the amount of knowledge he has. That realization should cause him to run to the open arms of the Saviour, to repent of his sin and receive forgiveness.

Jude's desire for Christians is that they develop discernment to be able to recognize false teachers for what they really are. With Jude's description of the character and conduct of apostate false teachers, there is no excuse for any Christian falling prey to those people and being seduced by their empty words.

6. SURVIVAL IN THE LAST DAYS

But you, beloved, ought to remember the words that were spoken beforehand by the apostles of our Lord Jesus Christ, that they were saying to you, "In the last time there shall be mockers, following after their own ungodly lusts." These are the ones who cause divisions, worldly minded, devoid of the Spirit. But you, beloved, building yourselves up on your most holy faith; praying in the Holy Spirit; keep yourselves in the love of God, waiting anxiously for the mercy of our Lord Jesus Christ to eternal life. And have mercy on some, who are doubting; save others, snatching them out of the fire; and on some have mercy with fear, hating even the garment polluted by the flesh.

Now to Him who is able to keep you from stumbling, and to make you stand in the presence of His glory blameless with joy, to the only God our Saviour, through Jesus Christ our Lord, be glory,

*majesty, dominion, and authority, before all time
and now and forever. Amen.*

Jude 17-25

Apostasy. False teachers. Deception. Lies. Falling
away from the faith. Rejecting the truth. God's
judgment. Hell. These are sobering realities with
which Jude has been confronting us. The most
natural human response to the thought of living
in an age characterized by apostasy which God
promises to punish severely is probably *fear.*

Though the major judgment and the punishment of hell will not take place until Christ's second coming, Christians living today are acutely
aware of the apostasy of the 20th-century church.
It is like standing in the center of a hurricane with
raging winds ripping apart everything around.

But Jude says that true Christians have nothing
to fear. Even as God ultimately judges and pun-
ishes false teachers, He continually protects and
ultimately guards Christians in the midst of such
a chaotic scene. Because humans often punish the
innocent along with the guilty, we sometimes forget that God knows how to make the distinction.
But He does, and we have an excellent example
of it in the Old Testament.

When Moses and Aaron confronted the Pharaoh
of Egypt and announced one devastating plague
after another, the Israelites were living in the land
of Goshen *right in the midst of Egypt.* Time after
time as the crippling plagues struck the Egyptians, God's chosen people were divinely protected. When the hail came, none fell in Goshen.
When the Egyptians' livestock died, no cattle died

in Goshen. When three days of absolute darkness hung over most of Egypt, the Israelites in Goshen had light. And finally when God struck down the firstborn in each Egyptian household, He gave instructions to the Israelites on how to remain safe by marking their doorposts with the blood of the Passover lamb. God made a clear distinction between Israel and Egypt, and He makes a similar distinction between believers and unbelievers today.

Unlike a human employer who puts blanket restrictions and sanctions on all his employees because he does not know which ones broke the rules, God knows who are the guilty ones and who are the innocent, and He is able to punish one group while blessing the other.

And this is what Jude teaches us in this last section of his letter—how to experience God's blessing on our lives as Christians even though we live in the midst of apostasy and judgment. Jude presents us with four specific instructions for survival: remember, remain, reach out, and rest.

Remember

This word, "remember" *mimnēskomai*, is the first imperative verb in the Book of Jude; and an imperative is a command. Jude instructs his readers to remember certain things. This is necessary because we naturally have a tendency to forget. Also, in the specific context of Jude, the pompous speeches of apostates and false teachers could cause Christians to forget the truth of God.

Jude wants Christians to remember first of all what apostasy is and that it will increase in the last days. He has described apostasy and the character of apostates: They defile the flesh, reject authority, and blaspheme glories; they promise much and deliver nothing; they lack spiritual life and fruitfulness; they are dead and useless, stirring up only filth and providing brief flashes of light which will soon vanish into eternal darkness. Jude has called to mind specific examples of apostasy from the Old Testament, examples with which his readers were familiar: the Israelites in the wilderness, the sinning angels, Sodom and Gomorrah, Cain, Balaam, and Korah. If any of Jude's readers had forgotten what the Scriptures taught about apostasy, they had now been clearly reminded.

Just as Jesus prepared His disciples for His death by telling them ahead of time what was going to happen, the apostles who wrote the New Testament prepared Christians to face the growing apostasy by predicting it. Jude's readers could have confidence in God's control, despite widespread apostasy. Without the prophecies in which God predicted apostasy, Christians, even today, might begin to think God was surprised that so many would reject His truth. But since God told us ahead of time, we can be assured that He is still in control of the situation—and we can put our faith and confidence in Him despite the "hurricane winds" around us.

Among the predictions we have are Paul's words to the Ephesian elders recorded in Acts 20:29-30: "I know that after my departure savage wolves will come in among you, not sparing the flock; and from among your own selves men will arise, speaking perverse things, to draw away the disciples after them." When the wolves in the Ephesian church began to attack the flock, Paul's preparation was a help to the Ephesian elders.

Another of Paul's predictions concerning apostasy is found in 1 Timothy 4:1: "But the Spirit explicitly says that in later times some will fall away from the faith, paying attention to deceitful spirits and doctrines of demons." And in a later letter to Timothy, Paul tells his young associate: "But realize this, that in the last days difficult times will come" (2 Tim. 3:1). The apostle then goes on (vv. 2-9) to list *in detail* the characteristics and methods of apostates.

Paul further prepared Timothy when he wrote: "For the time will come when they will not endure sound doctrine; but wanting to have their ears tickled, they will accumulate for themselves teachers in accordance to their own desires; and will turn away their ears from the truth, and will turn aside to myths" (2 Tim. 4:3-4).

The Apostle John warned: "Children, it *is* the last hour; and just as you heard that Antichrist is coming, even now many antichrists have arisen; from this we know that it is the last hour" (1 John 2:18). If "the last days" began with Jesus' first coming (Heb. 9:26), just think how much closer we are to the very end today, nearly 2,000 years later.

Jude's reference to "mockers" (v. 18) who follow their own ungodly lusts is similar to Peter's words: "Know this first of all, that in the last days mockers will come with their mocking, following after their own lusts" (2 Peter 3:3). In fact, the noun form for "mock" *empaiktēs* is found in only these two places in the New Testament and means "mocker." The more prevalent verb form contains the idea of playing a trick or deceiving someone.

These apostates are *pretenders* who play tricks with the Word of God and frequently try to pass themselves off as Bible teachers.

Jude says that these people cause "divisions" (v. 19), meaning they make false distinctions among Christians by elevating themselves above others. Those apostates saw themselves as the spiritual elite, superior to others in the church. At the love feasts they were probably in one of the cliques, separating themselves from those Christians they considered "inferior."

Greek philosophers taught that humans, animals, and plants all had soul life *psuchē*, and that only a few people rose above that level to attain spiritual life *pneuma*. Since apostates saw themselves as members of the spiritually elite, Jude's description of them as "worldly-minded" or "soulish" hurt.

Jude is saying that people who think they have risen to a high spiritual plane, and treat others as inferior, are the ones who have nothing in them but *psuchē* or soul life. In fact, Jude describes them as people dominated by their flesh, have no spiritual life or fruitfulness.

His last characterization of them—"devoid of the Spirit" (v. 19)—is the climax. A person who is devoid of the Spirit is not a Christian. "If anyone does not have the Spirit of Christ, he does not belong to Him" (Rom. 8:9). In pointing his finger at these apostates who consider themselves the ultimate in spirituality, Jude is making it clear that they are not even Christians.

Today we also see denominational leaders and presidents of Christian institutions and people who hold high positions in the church, but who are devoid of the Spirit. A member of my church once worked for a production studio in Hollywood which made church films for several major denominations. She painted a bleak picture of the spiritual condition of many church leaders with whom she had worked.

One man was known for drinking too much when he came to Los Angeles on business. Another church executive, who was known for removing his wedding ring en route to California, once listened as she described several exciting answers to prayer which she had received. He then confessed to her that he had never in his life gotten a specific answer to prayer and hardly knew what she was talking about. Both men were executives in their denominations, but were defiling the flesh and were apparently devoid of the Spirit.

To survive in these difficult times, Christians must *remember*. They must remember what apostasy is, and that it was long ago predicted and condemned. They must know God's Word in order to guard against growing apostasy.

Remain

In the midst of widespread apostasy, it is important for Christians to remain in the place which God says will be safe for them. Jude gives us another imperative, "Keep yourselves in the love of God" (v. 21), and then proceeds to tell us how to do just that.

"Keep" *tēreō* is the key verb in verses 20-21; the other three verbs ("building," "praying," and "waiting") are participles which describe or clarify the "keeping." This "keeping," in the Greek construction, relates to place or location "in the love of God," where we can receive His blessings.

In Jesus' Parable of the Prodigal Son, the father never changed in his attitude toward the son, but the son temporarily removed himself from the place where the father could bless him.

Similarly, there are times when I must discipline my children. I never stop loving them, but when they choose to disobey, they make it necessary for me to chastise rather than bless. As Christians, we are either in the place of blessing or the place of chastening. And Jude is telling us that it is especially important, in these difficult times, that we remain in the place where God can bless us.

Jude mentions three specific things we must do if we are to remain in the place of blessing.

1. Building. First, we are to *build* ourselves up on our most holy faith (v. 20). Christ, who is the Chief Cornerstone, laid the foundation for us, and now we who are living stones are to build upon it. After warning the Ephesian elders of the dangers of apostasy, Paul told them: "And now I commend you to God and to the Word of His grace, which is able to build you up and to give you the inheritance among all those who are sanctified" (Acts 20:32).

Studying the Word of God is like spiritual weight lifting. It makes us stronger and stronger, so we can stand firmly in the place of blessing and not be dragged or pushed out of it. When I played football, we had a really tough practice drill. One man would stand in a circle and the coach would send one other man (then two, then three, increasing each time) to try in about 30 seconds to move that man, by sheer brute force, out of the circle.

You had to be mighty strong to maintain your position when those heavy men hit you and began to drive you backward.

This pictures what Jude is driving at. Our faith, our confidence in God, will grow through our study and application of the Word of God to our lives so that we can maintain our position in the place of blessing—the center of God's will—during treacherous attacks.

2. *Praying.* The second thing we are to do to keep ourselves in the love of God is to *pray* in the Holy Spirit (v. 20). We should never allow ourselves to think we have become so spiritually strong that we no longer need to depend on God's strength. No matter how many theological answers we have, if we depend solely on our own strength, we will be pushed out of the circle.

The Apostle Paul describes the armor of God piece by piece (Eph. 6) and urges Christians to put on the whole armor. But then he immediately adds, "Pray at all times in the Spirit" (v. 18). Our warfare is not physical but spiritual, and prayer is essential to victory. Praying "in the Holy Spirit" is not some mystical or esoteric experience. And it has absolutely nothing to do with speaking tongues, as many people think. Praying in the Holy Spirit is like praying in the name of Jesus—it means praying according to the will of God (cf. Rom. 8:26-27).

3. *Looking.* Jude says we keep ourselves in the love of God by looking, or "waiting anxiously," for the mercy of our Lord Jesus Christ to eternal life. The compound, "waiting anxiously," has an intensified meaning. The same word is used in Titus 2:13: "Looking for the blessed hope and the ap-

pearing of the glory of our great God and Saviour, Christ Jesus."

Jude says we should live in eager anticipation of Christ's return. Waiting not for the judgment of the earth but for Jesus Himself, we are thus filled with hope. This expectant waiting helps to keep us in the love of God, the place of blessing, by purifying us (see 1 John 3:3).

All three of these modifying verbs are present tense participles, indicating that the actions they name should be *continuously* characterizing our lifestyle. In order to remain in the love of God and to survive in these last days of great apostasy, we should be continually studying the Scriptures, praying in the Spirit, and expectantly looking for the return of Christ.

Reach Out

Jude's next imperatives ("have mercy . . . save . . . have mercy," vv. 22-23) tell us that we should *reach out* to others, and this means evangelism. Because apostasy is so strong in these days, many are coming under the sway of false teachers. We must remind ourselves that God loves these people who are being victimized by these teachers. And because we have experienced the mercy of God, we may now show mercy to others by lovingly presenting the Gospel of Jesus Christ to them.

Christians need to *reach out* to three groups of people.

1. To sincere doubters. Sincere doubters ("some who are doubting") really do not know what is right or true. They are not antagonistic toward Christianity, but are just not sure. We often say of such people, "They are really open to the truth," but they are also usually open to untruth. While listening to the Gospel of Jesus Christ, they may also be listening to Jehovah's Witnesses or to Mormons.

Jude says we should show them "mercy" or "compassion" and aggressively reach out to draw them to the truth. We may need to share our own testimony with these doubters, or perhaps simply begin to spend time with them in order to help them find answers. Peter encourages us to be able to give reasons for our faith (1 Peter 3:15), so that we may help others come to faith in Christ.

2. *To endangered disbelievers.* Members of the second group are more committed to a form of false teaching and are thus closer to hell. In dealing with this group we cannot be shy or afraid of offending. Their false religious system is an offense to God, and unless we take a strong stand, we will not be able to rescue them out of the trap into which they have fallen.

Lot, Abraham's nephew, is a good example of a person being snatched from the fire. As God prepared to rain fire from heaven to destroy Sodom and Gomorrah, He sent two angels to rescue Lot and his family. When warned of the approaching judgment, Lot hesitated. But before he could linger long, the angels grabbed him, his wife, and his daughters and took them *forcibly* out of Sodom just before the city went up in flames.

Jude says these people are close to hellfire, and we must go after them with a sense of urgency. We must warn them of their great peril and try to get them away from the false teaching which will destroy them.

3. To confirmed sinners. The third group to whom we are to reach out is the most dangerous. Jude says we are to "have mercy with fear." This fear is associated with flight or running away, and means that we must be aware of the danger of temptation which may come to us.

This third group is made up of people who are already firmly entrenched in an evil system and have become propagators of it. It includes the apostate false teachers themselves. Christians must love these people while hating their wicked lifestyle and teaching.

Jude warns that we should even hate their garments which are polluted by sin. An Old Testament priest would examine an inner garment of a leper to detect the infection of leprosy. And if the garment had touched leprosy, it had to be burned. (See Leviticus 13:47-59.) Garments, in the Bible, often represent spiritual conditions. Christians, according to the Book of Revelation, will someday be clothed in white robes of righteousness.

Christians who seek to evangelize people in this third group need to be mature in their faith. They also need to realize the possibility of becoming confused in their own thinking, and consciously rely on the Holy Spirit for mental alertness, for spiritual perception, and for emotional stability. Satan is clever and powerful, and sharing Christ with people in this third group means interfering with what Satan considers *his* domain.

Because it is not too late for people from all three groups to be rescued from false doctrine and sin, Jude urges Christians to *reach out*! In such perilous times Christians are needed as rescuers, and are not to hide from needy people around them.

Rest

If Christians are to risk defilement and to live dangerously by trying to rescue people out of the very clutches of Satan himself, they might again be tempted to become fearful. They could fear that they would fall into sin or error or even into hell itself. Some Christians might wrongly worry that they might fall prey to apostasy or false teaching and lose their salvation.

After urging us to reach out to those in danger of hell, Jude reminds us again that there is no need for a committed Christian to fear. In fact, we can even *rest*, knowing that God is the One who keeps us safe. Jude refers to God as "Him who is able to keep you" (v. 24). Our great, omnipotent God is just as able to *keep* us as He was able to *save* us in the first place.

The word translated "keep" refers to watch-care in case of attack. So even if we come under attack from apostasy or Satan's legions in spiritual warfare, God is able to keep us from stumbling or falling into apostasy. We may sin or be deceived and lose the joy of our salvation or the blessings God wants to give us, but God is persistent in drawing us back to Himself. It is His desire for us to stand before His presence in heaven "blameless," clothed in the righteousness of Christ.

Peter describes Jesus Christ as "a Lamb unblemished and spotless" (1 Peter 1:19). Jude uses the same word (v. 24) to describe Christians. Christ sacrificed Himself for His church that He "might present to Himself the church in all her glory, having no spot or wrinkle or any such thing; but that she should be holy and blameless" (Eph. 5:27).

What joy we will experience as we are presented faultless in the very presence of God in heaven! And what wonderful joy springs to our hearts even now as we realize all that God has done, and is doing, for us.

Jude concludes his letter with praise: "To the only God our Saviour, through Jesus Christ our Lord, be glory, majesty, dominion, and authority, before all time and now and forever. Amen" (v. 25).

Jude's letter is a survival manual for Christians living in the midst of apostasy. Christians living in such an age should not be surprised by increasing apostasy. Through diligent study of God's Word, through praying in the Spirit, and through hopefully watching for the Lord's coming, Christians can confidently reach out to unbelievers with loving concern that they too may be saved.